GRAPHIS LOGO 1

KU-032-762

Has been made possible with the generous support of

The Strathmore Paper Company

This book is printed on Strathmore Writing Text,

Ultimate White, 80lb Weight

....

Wurdeermöglicht Durch die Grosszügige Unterstützung der

Strathmore Paper Company

Dieses Buch Wurde auf Strathmore Writing Text,

Hochweiss, 118g/m², Gedruckt

....

A pu Être Réalisé Grace au Généreux Soutien des

Papeteries Strathmore

Dieses Buch Wurde auf Strathmore Writing Text

Blanc. 118g/m²

GRAPHIS LOGO 1

The International Survey of Logo Design

Ein Internationaler Überblick über dei Gestaltung von Logos

Une vue d'ensemble de la Création Internationale de Logos

Edited by · Herausgegeben von · Réalisé par:

B. Martin Pedersen

Publisher and Creative Director: B. Martin Pedersen

Editor: Marisa Bulzone

Associate Editor: David Sassian

Designers: Adrian Pulfer, Mary Jane Callister, Eric Gillett

Graphis Press Corp., Zürich (Switzerland)

GRAPHIS PUBLICATIONS

GRAPHIS THE INTERNATIONAL BI MONTHLY JOURNAL OF VISUAL COMMUNICATION

GRAPHIS DESIGN THE INTERNATIONAL ANNUAL OF DESIGN AND ILLUSTRATION

GRAPHIS PHOTO THE INTERNATIONAL ANNUAL OF PHOTOGRAPHY

GRAPHIS POSTER THE INTERNATIONAL ANNUAL OF POSTER ART

GRAPHIS PACKAGING AN INTERNATIONAL SURVEY OF PACKAGING DESIGN

GRAPHIS DIAGRAM THE GRAPHIC VISUALIZATION OF ABSTRACT TECHNICAL
AND STATISTICAL FACTS AND FUNCTIONS

42 YEARS OF GRAPHIS COVERS AN ANTHOLOGY OF ALL GRAPHIS COVERS FROM 1944–86
WITH ARTISTS SHORT BIOGRAPHIES AND INDEXES OF ALL GRAPHIS ISSUES

GRAPHIS ANNUAL REPORTS AN INTERNATIONAL COMPILATION OF THE BEST
DESIGNED ANNUAL REPORTS

GRAPHIS CORPORATE IDENTITY AN INTERNATIONAL COMPILATION OF THE BEST IN
CORPORATE IDENTITY DESIGN

POSTERS MADE POSSIBLE BY A GRANT FROM MOBIL A COLLECTION OF 250 INTERNATIONAL
POSTERS COMMISSIONED BY MOBIL AND SELECTED BY THE POSTER SOCIETY

GRAPHIS-PUBLIKATIONEN

GRAPHIS DIE INTERNATIONALE ZWEIMONATSZEITSCHRIFT DER VISUELLEN KOMMUNIKATION

GRAPHIS DESIGN DAS INTERNATIONALE JAHRBUCH UBER DESIGN UND ILLUSTRATION

GRAPHIS PHOTO DAS INTERNATIONALE JAHRBUCH DER PHOTOGRAPHIE

GRAPHIS POSTER DAS INTERNATIONALE JAHRBUCH DER PLAKATKUNST

GRAPHIS PACKUNGEN EIN INTERNATIONALER UBERBLICK UBER DIE PACKUNGSGESTALTUNG

GRAPHIS DIAGRAM DIE GRAPHISCHE DARSTELLUNG ABSTRAKTER TECHNISCHER
UND STATISTISCHER DATEN UND FAKTEN

42 YEARS OF GRAPHIS COVERS EINE SAMMLUNG ALLER GRAPHIS UMSCHLAGE VON 1944–86
MIT INFORMATIONEN UBER DIE KUNSTLER UND INHALTSUBERSICHTEN ALLER
AUSGABEN DER ZEITSCHRIFT GRAPHIS

GRAPHIS ANNUAL REPORTS EIN INTERNATIONALER UBERBLICK UBER DIE GESTALTUNG
VON JAHRESBERICHTEN

GRAPHIS CORPORATE IDENTITY EINE INTERNATIONALE AUSWAHL DES BESTEN
CORPORATE IDENTITY DESIGN

POSTERS MADE POSSIBLE BY A GRANT FROM MOBIL EINE SAMMLUNG VON 250
INTERNATIONALEN PLAKATEN VON MOBIL IN AUFTRAG GEGEBEN UND VON DER
POSTER SOCIETY AUSGEWAHLT

PUBLICATIONS GRAPHIS

GRAPHIS LA REVUE BIMESTRIELLE INTERNATIONALE DE LA COMMUNICATION VISUELLE

GRAPHIS DESIGN LE REPERTOIRE INTERNATIONAL DE LA COMMUNICATION VISUELLE

GRAPHIS PHOTO LE REPERTOIRE INTERNATIONAL DE LA PHOTOGRAPHIE

GRAPHIS POSTER LE REPERTOIRE INTERNATIONAL DE L ART DE L AFFICHE

GRAPHIS EMBALLAGES LE REPERTOIRE INTERNATIONAL DES FORMES DE L EMBALLAGE

GRAPHIS DIAGRAM LA REPRESENTATION GRAPHIQUE DE FAITS ET DONNEES ABSTRAITS
TECHNIQUES ET STATISTIQUES

42 YEARS OF GRAPHIS COVERS RECUEIL DE TOUTES LES COUVERTURES DE GRAPHIS
DE 1944 86 AVEC DES NOTICES BIOGRAPHIQUES DES ARTISTES ET LE SOMMAIRE
DE TOUS LES NUMEROS DU MAGAZINE GRAPHIS

GRAPHIS ANNUAL REPORTS PANORAMA INTERNATIONAL DU DESIGN DE RAPPORTS
ANNUELS D ENTREPRISES

GRAPHIS CORPORATE IDENTITY PANORAMA INTERNATIONAL DU MEILLEUR DESIGN DE
L IDENTITE CORPORATE

POSTERS MADE POSSIBLE BY A GRANT FROM MOBIL UNE COLLECTION DE 250 AFFICHES
INTERNATIONALES COMMANDEES PAR MOBIL ET CHOISIES PAR LA POSTER SOCIETY

PUBLICATION NO 202 (ISBN 3 85709 429 X)
COPYRIGHT UNDER UNIVERSAL COPYRIGHT CONVENTION
COPYRIGHT 1991 BY GRAPHIS PRESS CORP 107 DUFOURSTRASSE 8008 ZURICH SWITZERLAND
JACKET AND BOOK DESIGN COPYRIGHT 1991 BY PEDERSEN DESIGN
141 LEXINGTON AVENUE NEW YORK NY 10016 USA

CONTENTS · INHALT · SOMMAIRE

AUSTRALIA · AUSTRALIEN · AUSTRALIE .... AUS

CANADA · KANADA · CANADA .... CAN

GERMANY · DEUTSCHLAND · ALLEMAGNE .... GER

GREAT BRITAIN · GROSSBRITANNIEN · GRANDE-BRETAGNE .... GBR

HUNGARY · UNGARN · HONGRIE .... HUN

IRAN · IRAN · IRAN.. IRN

ISRAEL · ISRAEL · ISRAEL.. ISR

ITALY · ITALIEN · ITALIE .... ITA

JAPAN · JAPAN · JAPON.. JPN

NETHERLANDS · NIEDERLANDE · PAYS-BAS .... NLD

POLAND · POLEN · POLOGNE .... POL

SOVIET UNION · SOWJETUNION · UNION SOVIÉTIQUE .... USR

SPAIN · SPANIEN · ESPAGNE... SPA

SWITZERLAND · SCHWEIZ · SUISSE .... SWI

TAIWAN · TAIWAN · TAIWAN .... TAI

TURKEY · TÜRKEI · TURQUIE .... TUR

USA · USA · ETATS-UNIS .... USA

YUGOSLAVIA · JUGOSLAWIEN · YOUGOSLAVIE .... YUG

REX PETEET

PHOTO BY DAVE BAUSMAN

In our studio's own promotional literature dealing with logos, we describe our approach to their design: logos are "puzzles of geometry, two–dimensional communications for multidimensional companies–all endeavor to capture the essence of a business, as simply as can be said." □ Although I have matured as a designer in the years since we wrote that copy, the statement remains for me true and basic to what makes a successful mark. I feel that in most instances simplicity will take care of timelessness, while capturing the essence of an enterprise or product will take care of appropriateness. □ But the quality that makes a mark most memorable and magical is the most difficult and elusive of all. It is present when a logo achieves all the above qualities, yet still manages to work on an underlying level that is not immediately apparent. It's a quality that involves the viewer. It's there, for instance, when you see a mark and instantly recognize the initials of the company–yet realize a moment later that they create a symbol or silhouette of that company's product or service. □ The logo I did for Lone Star Donuts, (Figure 3), a

Texas pastry baker, is one example of what I am describing. On first

glance you may simply see a single, "lone" star in a circle, which literal-

ly symbolizes the company name. On a second examination, however, you

discover that the mark is actually a silhouette of a donut and the star is

created by a stylized donut hole. The mark we did for Haggar Apparel,

(Figure 2), although appropriately much less whimsical, works in the

same fashion. You see the "H" and later you might interpret it as a

weave of fabric. Another example might be the mark for Mickey

Newberry, (Figure 5), a singer, songwriter, and composer. The unexpect-

ed arrangement of notes on a staff very naturally create an "N" while

capturing the essence of what the man does. □ Every logo can't do this,

and I believe it's not always even appropriate. Many times our firm has

come to the conclusion that initials, symbols, or a mark are not as suc-

cessful as a beautiful piece of type or a combination of type and silhou-

ette. These latter are alternatives to explore, and they become especially

attractive when the name is short, distinctive, recognizable, and has an

1

2

3

4

5

interesting combination of letter forms, as when a very natural ligature

can be considered because of the way two letters meet. For Mary Kay

Cosmetics, (Figure 1), we concluded that we needed it all. Because of the

diversity of applications, we needed the flexibility to create both a very

corporate feeling and a less formal, more fashionable look. The logotype

and the mark are used together or independently, depending on the situ-

ation. One last type of logo that I think can be successful doesn't neces-

sarily fall into the simplicity or longevity category, but rather uses detail

to communicate a mood, a feeling, or diversity. These marks are often

closely tied to fashion (for example, restaurants, apparel, furniture,

entertainment, etc.). They can become almost highly stylized illustra-

tions. The mark I designed for Mesa, (Figure 4), a Southwest furniture

and fine art gallery is a combination of typography and now ubiquitous

Southwest icons. The characters were reduced to their basic geometry

and the name allowed the typography to remain simple, yet distinctive,

without competing with the other elements. □ The best marks always look *so easy and natural. Not forced or contrived. Smart and streamlined.*

Unfortunately, they are almost never easy and usually require a multi-

tude of explorations beyond your eighth great idea. And, although this is

of course controversial, we welcome the client to see it all. After all,

they know their business better than we do. Clients have access to indus-

try imagery that we otherwise might miss. And, quite often, they have

very good ideas as well. Together, we begin to create a focus by eliminat-

ing the less successful (which is always obvious) or those that remind us

of something else we've seen. We have discovered that almost without

exception, the best will rise to the top. Occasionally, some gentle persuasion

may be necessary in the final choice between a good logo and a great logo.

REX PETEET, A DALLAS NATIVE, WORKED WITH SEVERAL PRESTIGIOUS ADVERTISING AND DESIGN FIRMS, INCLUDING THE THE RICHARDS GROUP AND PIRTLE DESIGN, PRIOR TO CREATING HIS OWN COMPANY WITH PARTNER DON SIBLEY EIGHT YEARS AGO. HE HAS WON NUMEROUS REGIONAL AND NATIONAL AWARDS, INCLUDING DALLAS, HOUSTON, LOS ANGELES, AND NEW YORK ART DIRECTORS SHOWS AND THE NATIONAL IABC COMPETITIONS. HIS WORK HAS BEEN PUBLISHED FREQUENTLY IN *CA* MAGAZINE AND THE NEW YORK ART DIRECTORS SHOW ANNUALS, AS WELL AS IN *PRINT* MAGA-ZINE, *PRINT* CASE BOOKS, AND THE *GRAPHIS* AND AIGA DESIGN ANNUALS. HE IS REPRESENTED IN THE PERMANENT COLLECTIONS OF THE LIBRARY OF CONGRESS AND THE MUSEUM OF MODERN ART IN HIROSHIMA, AND HIS WORK WAS INCLUDED IN THE UNITED STATES INFORMATION AGENCY'S EXHIBIT ON AMERICAN DESIGN THAT TOURED THE SOVIET UNION AND IN THE *GRAPHIS* 1988 50 POSTERS TOUR. MOST RECENTLY, HE WAS ONE OF SIXTEEN DESIGNERS REPRESENTING THE UNITED STATES IN THE INTERNATIONAL DESIGN WORLD'S MOST MEMORABLE POSTER 1990 INTERNATIONAL EXHIBITION IN PARIS. REX IS A BOARD MEMBER OF THE DALLAS SOCIETY OF VISUAL COMMUNICATIONS AND IS ONE OF THE FOUNDING MEMBERS OF THE TEXAS CHAPTER OF THE AMERICAN INSTITUTE OF GRAPHIC ARTS. REX ALSO JUDGES, LECTURES, AND TEACHES SEMINARS FOR VARIOUS INSTITUTIONS.

REX PETEET

In unserem eigenen Logobuch beschreiben wir Logos als "Geometrie-Puzzles, zwei-dimensionale Kommunikation für vieldimensionale Firmen. Sie sollen das Wesen eines Geschäfts so einfach wie möglich vermitteln." □ Ich bin, finde ich, als Designer reifer geworden seit jener Zeit, doch für mich ist diese Aussage noch immer richtig und grundlegend für ein erfolgreiches Firmen- oder Produktzeichen. Ich glaube, in den meisten Fällen wird Zeitlosigkeit durch Schlichtheit erreicht; Angemessenheit wird dadurch erzielt, indem wir das Wesen eines Produktes oder eines Unternehmens einfangen. □ Um ein Logo erinnerungswürdig zu gestalten und mit einem Hauch von Zauber zu umgeben, bedarf es aber eines weiteren Kriteriums - kaum definierbar und schwierig zu erreichen. Man erfüllt alle obengenannten Bedingungen und schafft gleichzeitig eine weitere, "versteckte" Ebene, die erst später entdeckt wird. Ein Logo, das diese Qualität aufweist, fordert und beschäftigt den Betrachter. Ein Beispiel dafür: Der Betrachter sieht ein Firmenzeichen und erkennt sofort die Initialen eines Unternehmens, einen Augenblick später erkennt er, dass das Zeichen das Symbol oder die Silhouette eines Produktes oder einer Dienstleistung des Unternehmens enthält. □ Das Logo, das ich für Lone Star Donuts, (Logo 3), eine Konditorei in Texas, entwarf, kann als Beispiel für den Prozess dienen, den ich beschreibe. Auf den ersten Blick sieht der Betrachter einen einzigen, "einsamen" Stern in einem Kreis, ein schlichtes Symbol, das den Namen des Unternehmens direkt überträgt. Schaut der Betrachter genauer hin, sieht er aber, dass das Firmenzeichen eigentlich die Umrisse eines Donuts und der Stern ein stilisiertes Donut-Loch darstellen. Unser Logo für Haggar Apparel, (Logo 2), obwohl nicht so offensichtlich zweischichtig, arbeitet mit ähnlichen Mitteln. Der Betrachter sieht ein "H", das er möglicherweise auch bei genauerem Hinsehen als ein Stück Stoff interpretieren könnte. Ein weiteres Beispiel könnte auch das Logo von Mickey Newberry, (Logo 5), sein, einem Sänger, Liederschreiber und Komponisten. Die überraschende Anordnung von Musiknoten auf einem Stab ergibt in natürlicher Weise ein "N", während das Logo zugleich darstellt, was dieser Mann macht. ▢ Nicht jedes Logo kann dies erreichen, und ich glaube, diese Form alleine wird auch nicht immer dem Produkt oder dem Unternehmen gerecht. Oft sind wir zum Schluss gekommen, dass Initialen, Symbole oder Zeichen nicht so erfolgreich sind wie ein wunderschöner Schriftzug oder eine Kombination von Schriftzug und Silhouette. Dies ist eine weitere Möglichkeit, die dann zum Tragen kommt, wenn der Name kurz, unverwechselbar und wieder-erkennbar ist, und eine interessante Kombination von Buchstabenformen enthält. So zum Beispiel, wenn sich eine Ligatur natürlich aufdrängt in der Art und Weise wie zwei Buchstaben miteinander verbunden werden, und dadurch ein einzigartiges

Logo entsteht. Das haben wir zum Beispiel für Mary Kay Cosmetics umgesetzt.

Wegen der Vielfalt der Produkte war es notwendig, genug Flexibilität zu haben, um

ein sehr starkes Corporate Feeling und einen weniger formellen Mode-Look zu schaf-

fen, der auch gewissen Produkten entspricht. Deshalb werden die Schriftzeichen des

Logos und das Produktzeichen zusammen benutzt und hängen - unabhängig von

einander - von der Situation ab. □ Eine letzte Kategorie von Logos, die erfolgreich

sein können, zeichnen sich nicht unbedingt durch Einfachheit und Zeitlosigkeit aus.

Vielmehr vermitteln sie durch Details eine Stimmung, ein Gefühl oder Gegensätze.

Solche Firmen oder Produktzeichen eignen sich jeweils eher für Modeströmungen

(z.B. Restaurants, Kleidung, Möbel, Unterhaltung usw.). Sie können auch stark stil-

isiert werden. Das Mesa-Firmenzeichen, das ich für eine Möbel- und Kunstgalerie im

Südwesten entworfen habe, ist eine Kombination von Typographie und Symbolen, die

in dieser Gegend allgegenwärtig sind. Die Buchstaben wurden auf die ihnen zugrun-

deliegende Geometrie reduziert, und dank dem Firmennamen konnte die

Typographie einfach, doch eigenständig behalten werden ohne Konkurrenz zwischen

Typographie und den einzelnen Buchstaben. □ Die besten Firmenzeichen sehen

immer einfach und natürlich und nie erzwungen oder künstlich aus. Leider sind sie

gewöhnlich nicht so einfach zu entwerfen und verlangen eine Menge Ideen neben den acht Vorschlägen, die man mehr oder weniger aus dem Ärmel schütteln kann. Wir

freuen uns auch, wenn der Kunde alle diese Ideen sieht. Dieses Vorgehen ist zwar

umstritten, aber wir haben herausgefunden, dass der Beitrag des Kunden sehr

wertvoll ist–schliesslich kennt er sein Geschäft besser als wir. Zudem hat er auch

Zugang zur Bildersprache seines Geschäftsbereichs, die wir vielleicht ausser Acht

lassen würden. Uns oft hat er auch sehr gute Ideen. Durch einen Ausscheidungsprozess

eliminieren wir die weniger erfolgversprechenden Ideen (die immer offensichtlich sind),

weil sie einen an etwas erinnern, das man bereits irgendwo gesehen hat, oder sie sind

aus andern Gründen nicht brauchbar. Wir haben gemerkt, dass die besten Logos zu

Top-Firmenzeichen werden–und da gibt es praktisch keine Ausnahmen. Manchmal

braucht es sanfte Überzeugungskünste, um den Unterschied zwischen einem guten

und einem grossartigen Logo herauszuschaffen Doch die Kunden respektieren dies.

Und ich glaube, das ist auch der Grund, warum sie überhaupt zu uns kommen.

REX PETEET, AUS DALLAS GEBÜRTIG, HAT FÜR VERSCHIEDENE BAKANNTE WERBEAGENTUREN UND DESIGN-FIRMEN GEARBEITET, U.A. FÜR THE RICHARDS GROUP UND PIRTLE DESIGN BEVOR ER VOR ACHT JAHREN MIT DON SIBLEY EINE FIRMA GRÜNDETE. ER HAT ZAHlREICHE REGIONALE UND NATIONALE AUSZEICHNUNGEN ERHALTEN: Z.B VON DEN ART DIRECTORS CLUBS AUS NEW YORK, DALLAS, HOUSTON UND LOS ANGELES UND DEN NATIONALEN IABC-WETTBEWERBEN. SEINE ARBEITEN WURDEN VERSCHIEDENTLICH IN DER ZEITSCHRIFT PRINT, IN DEN PRINT CASE BOOKS, IN GRAPHIS UND DEN AIGA DESIGN-JAHRBÜCHERN ABGEBILDET. ARBEITEN VON IHM BEFINDEN SICH IN DEN SAMMLUNGEN DER LIBRARY OF CONGRESS UND DES MUSEUM OF MODERN ART IN HIROSHIMA. BEI EINER WANDERAUSSTELLUNG ÜBER AMERIKANISCHES DESIGN, DIE VON DER UNITED STATES INFORMATION AGENCY IN DER SOWJETUNION ORGANISIERT WURDE, WAR ER EBENFALLS VERTRETEN, WIE AUCH IN DER GRAPHIS-WANDERAUSSTELLUNG DER 50 BESTEN PLAKATE 1988. ERST KÜRZLICH WAR ER EINER DER SECHZEHN DESIGNER, WELCHE DIE USA BEI DER INTERNATIONALEN PLAKATAUSSTELLUNG 1990 IN PARIS REPRÄSENTIERT HABEN. REX IST IM VORSTAND DER DALLAS SOCIETY OF VISUAL COMMUNICATIONS UND EINES DER GRÜNDUNGSMITGLIEDER DES AIGA IN TEXAS. ER IST IN VIELEN JURIES VERTRETEN, HÄLT VORLESUNGEN UND UNTERRICHTET AN VERSCHIEDENEN INSTITUTEN.

REX PETEET

Dans le volume que nous avons consacré à la promotion des logos issus de notre studio, nous définissons les logos comme suit: «Des puzzles géometrique. Des supports de commucication bidimensionnels pour des entreprises multidimensionnelles. Tous cherchent à incarner l'essence même d'une affaire, de manière aussi simple que possible.» □ *Je crois bien que j'ai mûri en tant que designer depuis le temps où nous avons réalisé cette promotion. Pourtant je crois que cette définition est restée aussi vraie et fondamentale qu'elle l'était alors, pour la création de marques à succès. J'estime que dans la plupart des cas la simplicité assure le caractère intemporel du logo et qu'il se montre d'autant plus approprié que son créateur réussit à lui faire exprimer l'essence même de l'entreprise ou du produit en question.* □ *Un autre critère contribue à rendre une marque mémorable, voire magique, et pourtant ce critère est le plus difficile à concevoir et à réaliser. Une fois les deux premiers critères satisfaits, le troisième intervient à un niveau sous-jacent qui ne se révèle qu'à l'usage. Il s'agit d'une qualité indissociable de l'observateur. Ainsi, lorsque vous apercevez un logo, vous reconnaissez immédiatement les initiales de l'entreprise en question; un instant après, vous réalisez que ces initiales composent un symbole ou une silhouette représentatif du produit ou du service en cause.* □ *Le logo que j'ai créé* pour *Lone Star Donuts*, *(Figure 3)*, *un pâtissier texan, peut illustrer ce que je suis en train de décrire. A première vue, il n'y a là qu'une étoile isolée (lone) inscrite dans un circle qui decrit la raison sociale de l'entreprise. Un second coup d'oeil vous apprend que la marque représente un fait la silhouette d'une beigne, l'etoile étant formée de manière stylisée par le trou de la rondelle. La marque que nous avons réalisée pour Haggar Apparel, (Figure 2), opère de manière identique, quoique nécessairement bien moins ingénieuse. Vous voyez le H, puis le découvrez un moment plus tard comme représentant une texture ou un tissu. Prenons encore un autre exemple, la marque pour le chanteur-compositeur Mickey Newberry (Figure 5). La disposition insolité des notes sur une portée crée tout naturellement un N tout en incarnant la nature même de l'artiste. □ Tous les logos ne sont pas aussi réussis, et ne s'accommodent pas forcément de cette approche. En de nombreuses occasions, notre société a découvert que les initiales, le symboles, les marques ne sont pas aussi efficaces qu'une composition typographique bien venue ou une combinaison de la typo avec une silhouette. C'est là une autre piste à explorer surtout lorsque le nom/la raison sociale est court, profilé, reconnaissable et qu'il présente une combinaison le lettres intéressante. C'est le cas par exemple lorsque la manière dont deux let-*

tres se jouxtent se prête à une forme de ligature tout naturelle, d'où un logo exceptionnel. Tel fut le cas de Mary Kay Cosmetics (Figure 1). En raison des applications trés variées de ce logo, il fallait être assez souple pour susciter en même temps une image institutionnelle forte et un look mode moins formel plus compatible avec certaine domaines d'utilisation. C'est pourquoi le logo et la marque s'utilisent conjointement ou independamment l'un de l'autre selon le besoins. ▫ Une dernière catégoire de logos qui peuvent connaître la succès ne rentrent pas nécessairement dans la famille de la simplicité ou de la longévité, mais servent plutôt à utiliser un détail pour créer une atmosphère, un sentiment ou une impression de diversité. Ce genre de marque est souvent intimement lié à la mode (restaurants, confection, ameublements, loisirs, etc.). Elle peut se meur en une illustration très stylisée. La marque que j'ai réalisés pour Mesa, (Figure 4), une galerie d'ameublements et de beaux-arts du Sud-Ouest, combine la typo et des emblèmes du Sud-Ouest désormais omniprésents. Les caractères sont réduits à leur tracé géométrique de base; la raison sociale a permis l'utilisation d'une typo simple quoique caractéristique, qui s'accorde avec l'ensemble. ▫ Les meilleures marques ont toujours l'air si simples, si naturelles. Pas forcées ou contraintes. Intelligentes, réduites à l'essentiel. Le malheur veut qu'elles ne soient presque jamais simples et requièrent généralement une foule d'explorations à partir de la huitième bonne idée. On peut être d'un avis différent, mais nous, on permet au client de voir tous ces essais successifs. Ça le met dans le bain. La contribution de client nous paraît irremplaçable; c'est qu'en fin de compte il connaît son affaire bien mieux que nous. Le client a un accès à l'imagerie industrielle que nous pouvons lui envier. Très souvent, il a de surcroît d'excellentes idées. En procédant par élimination, nous pouvons ensemble nous débarrasser des solutions moins efficaces, celles qui sont les premières à venir à l'esprit parce qu'elles nous rappellent autre chose, ou pour toute autre raison. Nous avons découvert—et c'est la régle quasi générale—que la meilleure solution finit toujours par s'imposer. De temps à autre, un gentil petit travail de persuasion établira la différence entre un bon logo et un logo exceptionnel. Les clients respectent cette approche. Je pense quant à moi que c'est la raison pour laquelle ils viennent nous trouver de préférence.

ORIGINAIRE DE DALLAS, **REX PETEET** A TRAVAILLÉ POUR DES AGENCES DE PUBLICITÉ PRESTIGIEUSES, PARMI LESQUELLES THE RICHARDS GROUP ET PIRTLE DESIGN, AVANT DE CRÉER, IL Y A HUIT ANS, SA PROPRE ENTERPRISE AVEC SON ASSOCIÉ DON SIBLEY. IL A REMPORTÉ DE MOMBREUX PRIX TANT À L'ÉCHELON RÉGIONAL QUE NATIONAL: IL FUR NATAMMENT LAURÉAT DES EXPOSITIONS DE L'ADC DE DALLAS, HOUSTON, LOS ANGELES ET NEW YORK ET DES CONDOURS NATIONAUX DE L'IABC. SES OEUVRES ONT SOUVENT ÉTÉ REPRODUITES DANS LE MAGAZINE *CA* ET DANS LES ANNUELS DU NEW YORK ART DIRECTORS SHOW, DANS LE MAGAZINE *PRINT* ET LES LIVRES DE ETTE ÉDITION, AINSI QUE DANS *GRAPHIS* ET AIGA DESIGN ANNUALS. IL EST REPRÉSENTÉ DANS LES COLLECTIONS PERMANENTES DE LA LIBRARY OF CONGRESS ET DU MUSÉ D'ART MODERNE D'HIROSHIMA. PAR AILLEURS, IL A PARTICIPÉ À L'EXPOSITION DE DESIGNAMÉRICAIN ORGANISÉE PAR L'INFORMATION AGENCY, QUI A FAIT LE TOUR DE L'URSS, ET À L'EXPOSITION ITINÉRANTE «50 AFFICHES GRAPHIS» EN 1988. RÉCEMMENT, IL A ÉTÉ L'UN DES SEIZE DESIGNERS SÉLECTIONNÉS POUR REPRÉSENTER LES ETATS-UNIS À L'EXPOSITION INTERNATIONALE DE LA MEILLEURE AFFICHE 1990 À PARIS. REX PETEET EST MEMBRE DE LA COMMISSION DE LA DALLAS SOCIETY OF VISUAL COMMUNICATIONS ET L'UN DES MEMBRES FONDATEURS DE LA SECTION DE L'AIGA DE DALLAS. AINSI DONC, IL EXERCE UNE ACTIVITÉ CRITIQUE, DONNE DES CONFÉRENCES ET ENSEIGNE DANS DE NOMBREUSES INSTITUTIONS.

KEN CATO

Terminology often gets in the way of clear communication. Logotype and logo *are words that are very loosely used in conversations between designers and business leaders. To me, a logotype is not a symbol. A logotype is the way the company name is expressed in type. It is one element in an identity system for a company, organization, or event, another element of which, usually, is the symbol.* □ *The symbol must be a visual expression of the essence of the corporation. It must be an expression of what the company does and the company attitude. Though it may be the focus, it, too, is but one element of a system. The way it's scaled to the surrounding components can have a dramatic effect on how it is perceived and the message it conveys.* □ *All the practical issues apply. Can the symbol be reproduced in a small size? In a single color? Will it translate well into signage or into three-dimensional form? But the most important attribute is ineffable–spirit. A spirit that allows extension. A spirit that can pervade a whole design program. The symbol should never be just a rubber stamp on a piece of stationery or something that's dropped into the corner of an advertisement.* □ *The symbol should also be easily recognized and, of course, memorable. Quite often the selection of the final design will be influenced by strategic considerations or a desire to capitalize on the uniqueness or inner strengths of the organiza-*

tion. □ Such was the case with Macquarie Bank (Figure 5). Here was a

company changing its name, adopting that of the first governor of

Australia, the man who introduced banking to the country. The final

design was a contemporary and abstract mark, but its inspiration was

the first currency developed in Australia—a Spanish silver coin with the

center punched out, yielding two denominations of currency. This gave

Australia the "Holey Dollar." It also gave us a symbol with a sense of

history determined the color in which it should run—silver. This bank

now has a five-year history and has recently produced scarves and ties

inspired by the symbol. □ More recently, a symbol was needed as a focus

for the effort to make Melbourne the site of the 1996 Olympic Games

(Figure 2). It was a two-fold effort: to convince the members of the

International Olympic Federation that Melbourne possessed the spirit of

the Olympic movement, and to inspire in its residents a sense that the

city was capable of staging the event. □ The 1996 games mark the one-

hundred year anniversary of the modern Olympiad. It was important to

develop a symbol that had a sense of history and at the same time was

contemporary. This was answered by the use of the Olympic flame ren-

1

2

3

4

5

dered in the traditional Olympic colors. The predictable and the famil-

iar, but presented in a new way–consequently a new and memorable

identity. The image was easily extended into three-dimensional form,

and when it was combined with the graphic interpretations of Olympic

sporting figures we had a total program. □ The Spoleto Arts Festival,

now known as the Melbourne International Festival of the Arts, decided

to adopt the traditional theater mask as a symbol, because of its univer-

sality (Figure 3). It came from us however, with a difference. It was

more abstract, more avant-garde, and very much reflected the attitude

of the festival and the events it presented. □ Once again, the symbol's

ability to be extended in other forms proved a real strength. Street festi-

vals and other activities provided opportunities for many interpreta-

tions of the concept–with theatrical makeup, for instance. □ The Applied

Research Corporation of Singapore advises industry of appropriate

areas of development to increase their competitiveness locally and over-

seas. The corporation's philosophical tenet is to inquire, to question. It

seemed logical to incorporate the question mark into their logotype

design. This somewhat esoteric yet central aspect of ARC's function is

projected through the simplicity of the three letters and a very accessi-

ble image (Figure 4). "Best of Best" is a simple concept. The company

selects the best product from many different categories. Out of an initial selec-

tion of quality products comes one ultimate choice. The symbol reflects this pro-

cess: an arrangement of incomplete seals of quality, with one complete seal

(Figure 1). The symbol is is easily extended to office signage, stationery, shop-

ping bags, and wrapping paper. The question of to what degree the client should

be involved in the development of a symbol is one that needs to be resolved early

in every program. The one absolute is a total commitment from top management

to the idea that a design program is necessary and will be supported. The ulti-

mate symbol and logotype solution will come only after the client and the design-

er full understand the characteristics and aims of the company, because if the

identity program is to be truly successful, its spirit must be reflected in every-

thing the company produces. The symbol must reflect the company's philoso-

phy, but the right symbol will, in turn, help keep that philosophy alive.

KEN CATO'S WORK HAS EARNED HIM AN INTERNATIONAL REPUTATION. MR. CATO IS CHAIRMAN OF CATO DESIGN PTY LIMITED, THE LARGEST DESIGN FIRM IN THE SOUTHERN HEMISPHERE, WITH OFFICES IN SYDNEY, PERTH, TOKYO, KUALA LUMPUR, HONG KONG, AUCKLAND, AND NEW YORK. A GRADUATE OF THE ROYAL MELBOURNE INSTITUTE OF TECHNOLOGY, MR. CATO IS A FOUNDING MEMBER AND FORMER CHAIRMAN OF THE AUSTRALIAN WRITERS AND ART DIRECTORS ASSOCIATION AND A MEMBER OF THE AMERICAN INSTITUTE OF GRAPHIC ARTS, ICOGRADA, AND DISENO GRAFICO ARGENTINA. HE IS THE FIRST AUSTRALIAN-BORN DESIGNER INVITED TO JOIN THE ALLIANCE GRAPHIQUE INTERNATIONALE. MR CATO'S WORK HAS BEEN WIDELY PUBLISHED. HE HAS BEEN THE SUBJECT OF A PORTRAIT IN *GRAPHIS* AND HAS ALSO BEEN FEATURED IN *IDEA* (JAPAN), *AUSTRALIAN BUSINESS*, *WORLD GRAPHIC DESIGN NOW*, AND *NOVUM GEBRAUCHSGRAPHIK*. HE WAS EDITOR OF *FIRST CHOICE*, A COMPILATION OF THE BEST WORK OF THE WORLD'S LEADING GRAPHIC DESIGNERS. MR. CATO IS A FREQUENT SPEAKER AT COLLEGES AND PROFESSIONAL SEMINARS, AND HE SERVES ON THE ADVISORY BOARDS OF A NUMBER OF EDUCATIONAL INSTITUTIONS. HE WAS A JUDGE FOR THE 1990 ANNUAL INTERNATIONAL EXHIBITION OF THE NEW YORK ART DIRECTORS CLUB. HIS OWN WORK HANGS IN SEVERAL INTERNATIONAL MUSEUMS AND HAS BEEN REPRESENTED IN EXHIBITIONS IN MANY COUNTRIES.

KEN CATO

Sehr häufig führt die Terminologie zu Kommunikationsproblemen. Das Wort Logo wird in Gesprächen zwischen Designern und Auftraggebern sehr locker verwendet. Für mich ist ein Logo kein Symbol. Mit Logo bezeichnet man den Schriftzug einer Firma. Es ist ein Element des Erscheinungsbildes einer Firma, einer Organisation oder einer Veranstaltung, zu dem als weiteres Element gewöhnlich das Symbol gehört. □ Das Symbol muss visueller Ausdruck des Wesens eines Unternehmens sein. Es muss Ausdruck der Tätigkeit und der Einstellung einer Firma sein. Obgleich es im Mittelpunkt stehen kann, ist auch das Symbol nur ein Element eines Systems. Das Verhältnis seiner Grösse zu den Elementen, die es umgeben, kann ausschlaggebend für die Wirkung und die Botschaft sein. □ Hier geht es um ganz pragmatische Fragen. Lässt sich das Symbol in kleinem Format wiedergeben? In nur einer Farbe? Lässt es sich als Schild oder dreidimensional verwenden? Aber das Allerwichtigste ist sein Geist, seine Ausstrahlung. Ein Geist, der sich auf anderes ausdehnen lässt. Ein Geist, der ein ganzes Design-Programm durchdringen kann. Das Symbol sollte in keinem Fall einfach ein Stempel auf Geschäftspapier sein oder etwas, das man in die Ecke einer Anzeige quetscht. □ Ein Symbol sollte leicht erkennbar und einprägsam sein. Oft sind strategis-

che Überlegungen oder der Wunsch, aus der Einzigartigkeit oder den inneren Stärken einer Firma Kapital zu schlagen, für die Wahl des endgültigen Designs ausschlaggebend. □ Das war zum Beispiel bei der Macquarie Bank der Fall (Logo 5). Das Unternehmen änderte seinen Namen, und zwar sollte es neu nach dem ersten Gouverneur Australiens, der das Bankwesen im Lande eingeführt hatte, benannt werden. Das endgültige Design bestand aus einem zeitgemässen, abstrakten Zeichen, aufgebaut jedoch auf der ersten in Australien entwickelten Währung–einer spanischen Silbermünze mit einem Loch in der Mitte. Damit erhielt Australien den «Loch-Dollar». Uns lieferte diese Münze ein Symbol mit geschichtlichem Hintergrund, und sie bestimmte die Farbe: Silber. Die Bank ist jetzt fünf Jahre alt. Kürzlich diente das Symbol sogar als Muster für Tücher und Krawatten, die sie herstellen liess. □ Ein noch aktuellerer Auftrag betraf den Entwurf eines Symbols für Melbournes Bewerbung um die Austragung der Olympischen Spiele im Jahre 1996 (Logo 2). Es ging dabei um zwei Dinge: die Mitglieder des Internationalen Olympischen Komitees zu überzeugen, dass Melbourne dem Geist der olympischen Bewegung entspricht und die Bewohner für die Sache zu begeistern. □ Mit den Spielen 1996 wird die moderne Olympiade 100 Jahre alt. Es war wichtig, ein Symbol zu entwickeln, das historisch und zeitgenössisch zugleich wirkt. Die Lösung war die Verwendung der olympischen

Flamme in den traditionellen olympischen Farben. Das Naheliegende und Vertraute, aber auf neue Art präsentiert–also eine neue und einprägsame Identität. Das Zeichen liess sich leicht in eine dreidimensionale Form umsetzten, und kombiniert mit graphischen Interpretationen der olympischen Sportarten ergab es ein vollständiges Programm. □ Die Organisatoren des Spoleto Arts Festivals, heute als «Melbourne International Festival of the Arts» bekannt, wählten die traditionelle Theatermaske wegen ihrer Allgemeingültigkeit als Symbol (Logo 3). Wir machten daraus jedoch etwas anderes. Es wurde abstrakter, mutiger. Dadurch wurde es dem Geist des Festivals und der Veranstaltungen gerecht. □ Auch in diesem Fall erwies es sich als Stärke des Symbols, dass es sich gut umsetzen liess. Strassenfeste und andere Aktivitäten boten ausreichend Gelegenheit, das Konzept auf verschiedenste Art zu interpretieren. □ Die Applied Research Corporation in Singapur berät Industrieunternehmen im Hinblick auf Expansionsmöglichkeiten, um so ihre Wettbewerbs-fähigkeit im In- und Ausland zu steigern. Es liegt im Wesen dieses Unternehmens zu fragen, in Frage zu stellen. Deshalb erschien es logisch, das Fragezeichen in das Firmenzeichen aufzunehmen. Dieser etwas esoterische, jedoch wichtige Aspekt von ARCs Tätigkeit wird durch die Schlichtheit der drei Buchstaben und in einem leicht zugänglichen Bild verdeutlicht (Figure 4). □ «Best of Best» ist ein einfaches Konzept. Die Firma wählt das beste Produkt in vielen verschiedenen Kategorien aus. Zuerst wird eine Reihe von Qualitätsprodukten zusammengestellt, und dann erfolgt die endgültige Auswahl. Das Symbol reflektiert diesen Prozess: Eine Ansammlung verschiedener unvollständiger Qualitätssiegel mit einem vollständigen Siegel (Logo 1). Das Symbol lässt sich leicht für Firmenschilder, Geschäftspapier, Tragtaschen und Einwickelpapier anwenden. □ Die Frage, in welchem Ausmass der Auftraggeber in die Entwicklung eines Symbols einbezogen werden soll, muss ganz zu Beginn der Arbeit geklärt werden. Voraussetzung ist die uneingeschränkte Einsicht und Zustimmung des Top Managements, dass ein Design-Programm notwendig ist, so dass das Projekt entsprechend unterstützt wird. Die endgültige Lösung für das Symbol und den Schriftzug wird erst gefunden, nachdem sich Auftraggeber und Designer vollkommen über Eigenschaften und Ziele der Firma einig sind, denn wenn ein Identitätsprogramm Erfolg haben soll, muss sein Geist in allem, was die Firma produziert, reflektiert werden. Das Symbol muss die Einstellung der Firma widerspiegeln, aber das richtige Symbol wird darüber hinaus dazu beitragen, das dieser Geist lebendig bleibt.

KEN CATOS ARBEITEN HABEN IHN AUF INTERNATIONALER EBENE BEKANNTGEMACHT. ER IST IM VORSTAND DER CATO DESIGN PTY LIMITED, DER GRÖSSTEN DESIGN-FIRMA DER SÜDLICHEN HEMISPHÄRE, MIT BÜROS IN SYDNEY, PERTH, AUCKLAND, TOKIO, KUALA LUMPUR, HONGKONG UND NEW YORK. ER HAT SEIN STUDIUM AM ROYAL MELBOURNE INSTITUTE OF TECHNOLOGY ABGESCHLOSSEN. KEN CATO IST GRÜNDUNGSMITGLIED UND EHEMALIGES VORSTANDSMITGLIED DER AUSTRALIAN WRITERS AND ART DIRECTORS ASSOCIATION, AUSSERDEM IST ER MITGLIED DES AMERICAN INSTITUTE OF GRAPHIC ARTS, DER ICOGRADA UND VON DISENO GRAFICO ARGENTINA. ER IST DER ERSTE GEBÜRTIGE AUSTRALIER, DER IN DIE ALLIANCE GRAPHIQUE INTERNATIONALE AUFGENOMMEN WURDE. KEN CATOS ARBEITEN WURDEN IN VIELEN ZEITSCHRIFTEN GEZEIGT; ES IST EIN PORTRÄT IN GRAPHIS ERSCHIENEN UND AUCH IDEA (JAPAN) AUSTRALIAN BUSINESS, WORLD GRAPHIC DESIGN NOW UND NOVUM GEBRAUCHSGRAPHIK HABEN ÜBER IHN BERICHTET. ER WAR HERAUSGEBER VON FIRST CHOICE, EINER ZUSAMMENSTELLUNG DER BESTEN ARBEITEN DER FÜHRENDEN GRAPHIK-DESIGNER AUS ALLER WELT.

KEN CATO

Les problèmes de terminologie viennent souvent compliquer la communication. Les mots logotype et logo sont employés de manière plutôt vague dans les conversations entre designers et dirigeants d'entreprise. Pour moi, un logotype n'est pas un symbole. Un logotype est la manière dont le nom de l'entreprise est exprimé typographiquement. C'est l'un des éléments du système d'identité commerciale d'une entreprise, d'une organisation ou d'une manifestation, le symbole constituant généralement le second élément. □ Le symbole doit être l'expression visuelle de la nature d'une société. Il doit être l'expression de ce que l'entreprise fait et de son attitude. Bien que ce soit le noyau, ce n'est cependant qu'un des éléments d'un système. La façon dont il s'harmonise avec les composantes annexes peut avoir un effet dramatique sur la manière dont il est perçu, ainsi que sur le message qu'il communique. □ Tous les aspects pratiques ont leur importance. Le symbole pourra-t-il être reproduit dans un petit format? en une seule couleur? Pourra-t-on le transposer sous forme d'enseigne ou en trois dimensions? Mais la qualité la plus importante est ineffable–il s'agit de l'esprit. Un esprit qui permette des prolongements. Un esprit qui peut envahir tout un programme de design. Le symbole ne devrait jamais être un simple tampon sur une

feuille de papier à lettres ou quelque chose qui soit relégué dans le coin

d'une publicité. □ Le symbole devrait également être aisément recon-

naissable et, bien sûr, facile à mémoriser. Il arrive assez fréquemment

que le choix définitif soit influencé par des considérations stratégiques

et un désir d'exploiter l'unicité ou les forces inhérentes à l'organisa-

tion. □ Ce fut le cas avec la banque australienne Macquarie Bank

(Figure 5). Nous avions là affaire à une société qui changeait de nom,

adoptant celui du premier gouverneur du pays, l'homme qui introduisit

le système bancaire sur ce continent. Le projet définitif se présentait

comme une marque contemporaine et abstraite, mais il s'inspirait de la

première monnaie à avoir été introduite en Australie—une pièce

d'argent espagnole avec un poinçon au centre, comportant deux dénom-

inations de cette monnaie. C'est ainsi que l'Australie eut son "Holey

Dollar". Cela nous donna aussi un symbole chargé d'histoire et déter-

mina la couleur dans laquelle il devrait être réalisé - l'argent.

Maintenant, cette banque existe depuis cinq ans et dernièrement, elle a

produit des foulards et des cravates inspirés de ce symbole. □ Plus *récemment, on nous demanda un symbole concentré sur l'image de Melbourne, site des Jeux Olympiques de 1996 (Figure 2). Notre tâche fut double: il nous fallut d'une part convaincre les membres de la Fédération olympique internationale que Melbourne possédait bien l'esprit du mouvement olympique, et d'autre part, suggérer à ses habitants que la ville allait être capable d'organiser cette manifestation.* □ *Les Jeux de 1996 marquent le centième anniversaire des Olympiades modernes. Il était important d'élaborer un symbole qui ait une dimension historique et qui, en même temps, soit d'actualité. On utilisa donc, chose prévisible, la flamme olympique dans les couleurs traditionnelles; cependant, ce motif bien connu était présenté d'une nouvelle manière–en l'occurrence, une identité nouvelle et facile à mémoriser. L'image pouvait être facilement agrandie sous forme d'objet tridimensionnel et, une fois combinée aux interprétations graphiques des sportifs olympiques, nous avions un programme complet.* □ *Le Festival artistique de Spoleto, aujourd'hui connu sous le nom de Festival artistique international de Melbourne, décida d'adopter comme symbole le traditionnel masque de théâtre, à cause de son universalité (Figure 3).*

Mais celui que nous avons créé était quand même différent. Il est plus abstrait, d'avant-garde, et il reflète nettement mieux l'esprit du festival et les manifestations qui y sont présentées. □ Une fois de plus, la possibilité d'étendre le symbole à d'autres formes fit réellement ses preuves. Des festivals de rue et autres activités fournirent l'occasion d'interpréter le concept de diverses manières—avec un maquillage de scène par exemple. □ La Applied Research Corporation (A.R.C.) de Singapour conseille aux industries des aires de développement appropriées afin qu'elles puissent accroître leur compétitivité à l'échelle locale et internationale. La philosophie de cette société se résume ainsi: enquêter, questionner. Il paraissait donc logique d'incorporer le point d'interrogation dans le design du logo. Cet aspect central, bien que quelque peu ésotérique, de la fonction d'A.R.C. s'exprime au travers de la simplicité des trois lettres, une image à la portée de tous (Figure 4). □ "Best of Best" est un concept fort simple. La société sélectionne ce qui se fait de meilleur dans diverses catégories. Le choix définitif s'opère à partir d'une sélection initiale de produits de qualité. Le symbole reflète ce processus: un assemblage de labels de qualité incomplets, un seul étant reproduit dans son intégralité (Figure 1). Le symbole peut être aisé-ment repris sur les bâtiments administratifs, sur le papier à lettres, les sacs à commissions ou le papier d'emballage. □ La question de savoir jusqu'à quel point le client doit être impliqué dans la conception du symbole doit être résolue assez tôt pour chaque programme. Une chose essentielle, c'est l'engagement total et l'appui de la direction quant à la nécessité d'un programme de design. La solution définitive du symbole et du logotype viendra seulement une fois que le client et le designer auront pleinement compris les caractéristiques et les objectifs de l'entreprise; en effet, pour que le programme d'identité soit vraiment réussi, il faut qu'il reflète l'esprit dans lequel l'entreprise produit et sa philosophie, mais le vrai symbole devra, à son tour, aider à perpétuer cette philosophie.

L'ŒUVRE DE **KEN CATO** LUI A VALU UNE RÉPUTATION INTERNATIONALE. KEN CATO EST PRÉSIDENT DE CATO DESIGN PTY LIMITED, LA PLUS GRANDE FIRME DE DESIGN DE L'HÉMISPHERE SUD, AVEC DES BUREAUX À SYDNEY, PERTH, AUCKLAND, TOKYO, KUALA LUMPUR, HONG KONG ET NEW YORK. DIPLOMÉ DU ROYAL MELBOURNE INSTITUTE OF TECHNOLOGY, KEN CATO EST MEMBRE FONDATEUR ET ANCIEN PRÉSIDENT DE L'ASSOCIATION DES ÉCRIVAINS ET DIRECTEURS ARTISTIQUES AUSTRALIENS; IL EST ÉGALEMENT MEMBRE DE L'AMERICAN INSTITUTE OF GRAPHIC ARTS, D'ICOGRADA ET DE DISENO GRAFICO ARGENTINA. IL FUT LE PREMIER DESIGNER NÉ EN AUSTRALIE INVITÉ À FAIRE PARTIE DE L'ALLIANCE GRAPHIQUE INTERNATIONALE. L'ŒUVRE DE KEN CATO A ÉTÉ LARGEMENT PUBLIÉE. ON A PRÉSENTÉ SON PORTRAIT DANS *GRAPHIS* ET IL A FAIT ÉGALEMENT L'OBJET D'UNE ÉTUDE DANS *IDEA* (JAPON), *AUSTRALIAN BUSINESS*, *WORLD GRAPHIC DESIGN NOW* ET *NOVUM GEBRAUCHSGRAPHIK*. IL FUT ÉDITEUR DE *FIRST CHOICE*, UNE COMPILATION DES MEILLEURS TRAVAUX DES PRINCIPAUX GRAPHIC DESIGNERS DU MONDE ENTIER. KEN CATO DONNE SOUVENT DES CONFÉRENCES DANS DES UNIVERSITÉS ET DIRIGE DES SÉMINAIRES PROFESSIONNELS; IL EST ÉGALEMENT DANS LE JURY CON-SULTATIF D'UN GRAND NOMBRE D'ÉCOLES. IL A FAIT PARTIE DU JURY DE L'EXPOSITION INTERNA-TIONALE ANNUELLE 1990 DU NEW YORK ART DIRECTORS CLUB. SES ŒUVRES SONT ACCROCHÉES DANS PLUSIEURS GRANDS MUSÉES INTERNATIONAUX ET ELLES ONT ÉTÉ EXPOSÉES DANS DE NOMBREUX PAYS.

CREATIVE

CREATIVE

CRÉATIFS

1

■ 1. DESIGN FIRM: FRESH PRODUCE STUDIO ART DIRECTORS: PAMELLA GECAN/THOMAS GECAN
DESIGNERS: PAMELLA GECAN/THOMAS GECAN/DIANA HASSELL ILLUSTRATOR: THOMAS GECAN (USA)

1

■ 1. DESIGN FIRM: BRADBURY DESIGN ART DIRECTOR/DESIGNER: CATHARINE BRADBURY (CAN) ■ 2. DESIGN FIRM: TRADEMARK DESIGN LTD. ART DIRECTOR/DESIGNER: CLIVE GAY (GBR) ■ 3. DESIGN FIRM: THE DUFFY DESIGN GROUP ART DIRECTOR/DESIGNER: CHARLES S. ANDERSON ILLUSTRATORS: CHARLES S. ANDERSON/LYNN SCHULTE (USA) ■ 4. DESIGN FIRM: MANHATTAN DESIGN DESIGNERS: PAT GORMAN/FRANK OLINSKY (USA) ■ 5. DESIGN FIRM: JACK TOM DESIGN ART DIRECTOR/DESIGNER/ILLUSTRATOR: JACK TOM (USA)

Ⓣ R A D E M A R K

2

3

4

5

1

2

■ **1-4.** DESIGN FIRM: RICKABAUGH GRAPHICS ART DIRECTOR: ERIC RICKABAUGH DESCRIPTION: (#3) FOR THE FIRM'S LINE OF DESIGN PRODUCTS FOR RETAIL/FÜR EINE LINIE VON FÜR DEN VERKAUF BESTIMMTEN DESIGNER-PRODUKTEN DIESER FIRMA/POUR LA GAMME DE PRODUITS DESIGN DE CETTE ENTREPRISE (USA)

3

4

1

2

3

4

5

■ 1. DESIGN FIRM: YEE-PING CHO ART DIRECTOR/DESIGNER: YEE-PING CHO (USA) ■ 2. DESIGN FIRM: PAUL
CURTIN DESIGN ART DIRECTOR: PAUL CURTIN DESIGNER: PETER LOCKE (USA) ■ 3. DESIGN FIRM: MINORU
MORITA GRAPHIC DESIGN ART DIRECTOR/DESIGNER: MINORU MORITA (USA) ■ 4. DESIGN FIRM: DAVID
VOGLER DESIGN ART DIRECTOR/DESIGNER: DAVID VOGLER HAND LETTERING: RAY BARBER (USA) ■ 5. DESIGN
FIRM: CHARLES S. ANDERSON DESIGN CO. ART DIRECTOR/DESIGNER/ILLUSTRATOR: CHARLES S. ANDERSON (USA)

1

■ 1. DESIGN FIRM: DAVID TILLINGHAST ILLUSTRATION ART DIRECTOR/DÉSIGNER: DAVID TILLINGHAST (USA)
■ 2. CLIENT: LENNON & BAUSMAN DESIGN FIRM: THE DUFFY DESIGN GROUP ART DIRECTOR: CHARLES S.
ANDERSON DESIGNER: SARA LEDGARD ILLUSTRATOR: LYNN SCHULTE (USA) ■ 3.CLIENT: SIDNEY COOPER
DESIGN FIRM: MARGO CHASE DESIGN ART DIRECTOR/DESIGNER: MARGO CHASE (USA) ■ 4. CLIENT: GUY
HURKA DESIGN FIRM: SOL COMMUNICATIONS ART DIRECTOR/DESIGNER/ILLUSTRATOR: CARLOS SEGURA (USA)

2

3

4

1

2

3

■ **1.** CLIENT: CURTIN EMERSON RANSICK ADVERTISING DESIGN FIRM: PAUL CURTIN DESIGN ART DIRECTOR: PAUL CURTIN DESIGNER: LESLIE DRESSEL DESCRIPTION: FOR AN ADVERTISING FIRM/FÜR EINE WERBEAGENTUR/POUR UNE AGENCE DE PUBLICITÉ (USA) ■ **2.** DESIGN FIRM: TERRY O COMMUNICATIONS ART DIRECTOR/DESIGNER: TERRY O'CONNOR (CAN) ■ **3.** CLIENT: SOLO EDITIONS DESIGN FIRM: THE PUSHPIN GROUP ART DIRECTOR: SEYMOUR CHWAST DESIGNER: GREG SIMPSON DESCRIPTION: FOR AN ADVERTISING AGENCY WHOSE CLIENTS ARE PHOTOGRAPHERS, ILLUSTRATORS, ARTISTS' REPRESENTATIVES, AND ART GALLERIES/FÜR EINE WERBEAGENTUR, DEREN KUNDEN PHOTOGRAPHEN, ILLUSTRATOREN, KÜNSTLER-AGENTUREN UND KUNSTGALERIEN SIND/POUR UNE AGENCE DE PUBLICITÉ QUI A POUR CLIENTS DES PHOTOGRAPHES, ILLUSTRATEURS, AGENCES ARTISTIQUES ET GALERIES D'ART (USA)

4

5

6

■ **4.** CLIENT: BUSINESS WEEK CORPORATE ADVERTISING DESIGN FIRM: DESIGN CENTER ART DIRECTOR: JOHN REGER DESIGNERS: DAN OLSON/KOBE DESCRIPTION: FOR A BUSINESS MAGAZINES'S CORPORATE ADVERTISING OFFICE/FÜR DIE WERBEABTEILUNG EINES WIRTSCHAFTSMAGAZINS/POUR LE DÉPARTEMENT PUBLICITÉ D'UN MAGAZINE ÉCONOMIQUE (USA) ■ **5.** CLIENT: OBUNSHA LTD. DESIGN FIRM: ROBERT MILES RUNYAN & ASSOCIATES ART DIRECTOR/DESIGNER: JIM BERTÉ DESCRIPTION: FOR A COMMUNICATIONS FIRM/FÜR EINE KOMMUNIATIONS-FIRMA/POUR UNE SOCIÉTÉ DE COMMUNICATION (JPN) ■ **6.** CLIENT: JANET VIRNIG, ARTIST'S REP DESIGN FIRM: GRANDPRÉ AND WHALEY, LTD ART DIRECTOR/DESIGNER: KEVIN WHALEY (USA)

POLYGON PICTURES

1

2

3

4

■ 1. CLIENT: POLYGON PICTURES DESIGN FIRM: IGARASHI STUDIO ART DIRECTOR: TAKENOBU IGARASHI DESIGNER: YUKIMO SASAGO (JPN) ■ 2. CLIENT: CROSSROAD FILMS DESIGN FIRM: PENTAGRAM DESIGN ART DIRECTOR: WOODY PIRTLE DESIGNERS: WOODY PIRTLE/JENNIFER LONG (USA) ■ 3. CLIENT: THE GREAT ELECTRICAL MOTION PICTURE PRODUCTION CO. DESIGN FIRM: BRADBURY DESIGN ART DIRECTOR/DESIGNER: CATHARINE BRADBURY (CAN) ■ 4. CLIENT: ONTARIO CINECORP. DESIGN FIRM: BURNS & CO. ART DIRECTOR/DESIGNER: ROBERT BURNS (CAN) ■ 5. CLIENT: TRANQUILO PRODUCTIONS DESIGN FIRM: THE GRAPHIC DESIGN GROUP OF ALBERT C. MARTIN & ASSOCIATES ART DIRECTORS/DESIGNERS: KEVIN CONSALES/SUSAN VINIK (USA)

Rufglen Films

1

■ 1. CLIENT: RUFGLEN FILMS/DEMI MOORE ART DIRECTOR: ROD DYER DESIGNER: HARRIET BREITBORDE (USA) ■ 2. CLIENT: DOUG BUTTLEMAN FOR THE RIVERDOGS DESIGN FIRM: MARGO CHASE DESIGN ART DIRECTOR/DESIGNER: MARGO CHASE DESCRIPTION: FOR A ROCK BAND/FÜR EINE ROCK-BAND/POUR UN GROUPE DE ROCK (USA) ■ 3. CLIENT: 3RD STREET SOUND DESIGN FIRM: JOE BARATELLI ART DIRECTOR/DESIGNER: JOE BARATELLI DESCRIPTION: RECORDING STUDIO/AUFNAHME-STUDIO/STUDIO D'ENREGISTREMENT (USA) ■ 4. CLIENT: GEFFEN RECORDS DESIGN FIRM: MARGO CHASE DESIGN ART DIRECTOR: GABRIELLE RAUMBERGER DESIGNER: MARGO CHASE DESCRIPTION: FOR AN ALBUM RELEASE/FÜR EINE NEUE SCHALLPLATTE/POUR UN NOUVEAU DISQUE (USA)

2

3

4

M1ke+The MeChaN1C5

1

2

■ 1. CLIENT: MIKE RUTHERFORD/HIT & RUN MUSIC DESIGN FIRM: HALAN GREY VERMEIR ART DIRECTOR/DESIGNER: GEOFF HALPIN DESCRIPTION: ROCK BAND/ROCK-BAND/GROUPE DE ROCK (GBR)
■ 2. CLIENT: CBS/SONY RECORDS ART DIRECTOR/DESIGNER: KEISUKE UNOSAWA DESCRIPTION: FOR THE POP STAR MARTIKA/FÜR DEN POP-STAR MARTIKA/POUR LA VEDETTE DU POP MARTIKA (JPN)

PROFESSIONALS

DIENSTLEISTUNGEN

PROFESSIONNELS

1

■ 1. CLIENT: PARKLAND HOSPITAL DESIGN FIRM: RICHARD BROCK MILLER MITCHELL & ASSOC. ART DIRECTOR/DESIGNER: DANNY KAMERATH DESCRIPTION: HOSPITAL PEDIATRIC TRAUMA CENTER/FÜR DAS PÄDIA-TRISCHE TRAUMA-ZENTRUM EINES SPIITALS/CENTRE DE TRAUMATOLOGIE PÉDIATRIQUE D'UN HOPITAL (USA)

1

2

3

■ **1.** Client: CARE MANAGEMENT, INC. Design Firm: LAUREN SMITH DESIGN Art Director/Designer: LAUREN SMITH Description: FOR A NURSING CARE CORPORATION/FÜR EIN KRANKENPFLAGE-UNTERNEHMEN/POUR UNE ENTREPRISE DE SOINS INFIRMIERS (USA) ■ **2.** Client: MEDICAL INNOVATION CAPITAL, INC. Design Firm: THE DUFFY DESIGN GROUP Art Director/Designer: CHARLES S. ANDERSON Illustrators: CHARLES S. ANDERSON/LYNN SCHULTE Description: MEDICAL FINANCIAL SERVICES/FINANZIERUNGEN IM MEDIZINISCHEN BEREICH/FINANCEMENT DE PRESTATIONS MÉDICALES (USA) ■ **3.** Client: PLANO CRISIS CENTER Design Firm: PETERSON & COMPANY Art Directors: SCOTT RAY/ARTHUR EISENBERG Description: FOR A CRISIS HOTLINE CENTER/FÜR EIN KRISEN-NOTFALLZENTRUM/POUR UN CENTRE D'URGENCES (USA)

4

5

6

■ **4.** CLIENT: PHARMACEUTICAL ROUND TABLE DESIGN FIRM: COLVIN RATTAN DESIGN ART DIRECTOR/DESIGNER: ALAN COLVIN (USA) ■ **5.** CLIENT: MEDICAL INNOVATION CAPITAL, INC. DESIGN FIRM: THE DUFFY DESIGN GROUP ART DIRECTOR/DESIGNER: CHARLES S. ANDERSON ILLUSTRATORS: CHARLES S. ANDERSON/LYNN SCHULTE DESCRIPTION: MEDICAL FINANCIAL SERVICES/ FINANZIERUNGEN IM MEDIZINISCHEN BEREICH/FINANCEMENT DE PRESTATIONS MÉDICALES (USA) ■ **6.** CLIENT: MOBILITY FOUNDATION DESIGN FIRM: RICHARD BROCK MILLER MITCHELL & ASSOC. ART DIRECTOR/DESIGNER: STEVE MILLER DESCRIPTION: FOR AN ORGANIZATION DEDICATED TO HELPING PARAPLEGICS OVERCOME THEIR DISABILITIES/FÜR EINE ORGANISATION, DIE SICH UM PARAPLEGIKER KÜMMERT/POUR UNE ORGANISATION D'AIDE AUX PARAPLÉGIQUES (USA)

1

2

3

SAMARITAN

4

5

6

■ **1.** CLIENT: KANE HOSPITAL DESIGN FIRM: AGNEW MOYER SMITH, INC. DESIGNER: DON MOYER DESCRIPTION: FOR A HOSPITAL'S REGIONAL CENTERS/FÜR DIE REGIONALEN ZENTREN OINES SPITALS/POUR LES CENTRES RÉGIONAUX D'UN HOPITAL (USA) ■ **2.** CLIENT: IKTISAT BANKASI AGENCY: REKLAMEVI YOUNG & RUBICAM ART DIRECTOR/DESIGNER: BÜLENT ERKMEN DESCRIPTION: FOR A BANK/FÜR EINE BANK/POUR UNE BANQUE (TUR) ■ **3.** CLIENT: HOSPITAL MOVIES DESIGN FIRM: KNAPE & KNAPE ART DIRECTOR/DESIGNER: MICHAEL CONNORS DESCRIPTION: FOR A COMPANY THAT RENTS MOVIES TO HOSPITAL PATIENTS/FÜR EINE FIRMA, DIE FILME AN PATIENTEN IN KRANKENHÄUSERN AUSLEIHT/POUR UNE SOCIÉTÉ DE LOCATION DE FILMS AUX PERSONNES HOSPITALISÉES (USA) ■ **4.** CLIENT: THE SAMARITAN FOUNDATION DESIGN FIRM: SBG PARTNERS ART DIRECTORS: NICOLAS SIDJAKOV/JERRY BERMAN DESIGNER: JACKIE FOSHAUG (USA) ■ **5.** CLIENT: ARIZONA COMMERCE BANK DESIGN FIRM: HUBBARD AND HUBBARD DESIGN ART DIRECTOR/DESIGNER: ANN MORTON HUBBARD DESCRIPTION: FOR A COMMERCIAL BANK/FÜR EINE HANDELSBANK/POUR UNE BANQUE COMMERCIALE (USA) ■ **6.** CLIENT: FIRST BANK DESIGN FIRM: CHARLES S. ANDERSON DESIGN CO. ART DIRECTOR/DESIGNER: CHARLES S. ANDERSON DESCRIPTION: LOGO FOR THE BANK'S ANNUAL PARTNERSHIP CONFERENCE/LOGO FÜR DIE JÄHRLICHE GESELLSCHAFTER-SITZUNG EINER BANK/LOGO POUR L'ASSEMBLÉE ANNUELLE DES SOCIÉTAIRES D'UNE BANQUE (USA)

CONSULTANT
CONFERENCE

1

2

3

MITCHELL PHOENIX

4

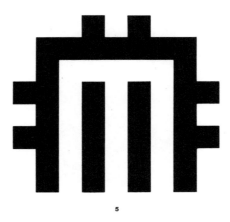

5

■ **1.** CLIENT: NOVELL, INC. ART DIRECTORS: LISA HILLDEBRAND/JILL BUSTAMANTE DESIGNER: JILL BUSTAMANTE DESCRIPTION: LOGO FOR A CONSULTANTS' CONFERENCE/LOGO FÜR EINE BERATER-KONFERENZ LOGO POUR UNE CONFÉRENCE DE CONSEILS D'ENTREPRISES (USA) ■ **2.** CLIENT: GILBERT PAPER DESIGN FIRM: SAMUEL KUO DESIGN ART DIRECTOR/DESIGNER: SAMUEL KUO DESCRIPTION: FOR A COMPUTER DATING COMPANY/FÜR EINE COMPUTER-PARTNERVERMITTLUNGS-FIRMA/POUR UNE AGENCE MATRIMONILALE UTILISANT L'ORDINATEUR (USA) ■ **3.** CLIENT: REBO RESEARCH, INC. DESIGN FIRM: M PLUS M INCORPORATED ART DIRECTORS: MICHAEL MCGINN/TAKAAKE MATSUMOTO DESIGNER: MICHAEL MCGINN ILLUSTRATOR: JACK TOM DESCRIPTION: LOGO FOR A TWO-WAY FIBER OPTIC TRANS-MISSION SYSTEM/LOGO FÜR EIN OPTISCHES UEBERMITTLUNGSSYSTEM MIT ZWEI FASERN/LOGO POUR UN SYSTEME DE TRANSMISSION OPTIQUE À DEUX FIBRES (USA) ■ **4.** CLIENT: MITCHELL PHOENIX LTD DESIGN FIRM: HALPIN GREY VERMEIR ART DIRECTORS: JOHN GREY/PIERRE VERMEIR DESIGNER: DAVID JAMES DESCRIPTION: MANAGEMENT TRAINING CONSULTANTS/KADERSCHULUNG/FORMATION DE CADRES (GBR) ■ **5.** CLIENT: MIMAR-LAR A.S. ART DIRECTOR/DESIGNER: BÜLENT ERKMEN DESCRIPTION: FOR AN ARCHITECTURE FIRM/FÜR EIN ARCHITEKTUR-BÜRO/POUR UN BUREAU D'ARCHITECTES (TUR)

1

■ **1.** CLIENT: KEENAN LAND COMPANY DESIGN FIRM: TOLLESON DESIGN ART DIRECTOR/DESIGNER: STEVEN TOLLESON DESCRIPTION: FOR HOLLIS STREET, A RETAIL DEVELOPMENT/LOGO FÜR HOLLIS STREET, EINE LADENSTRASSE/POUR HOLLIS STREET, UNE RUE COMMERÇ*NTE (USA) ■ **2.** CLIENT: SANTA FE INTERNATIONAL CORPORATION DESIGN FIRM: JANN CHURCH PARTNERS ART DIRECTOR/DESIGNER: JANN CHURCH DESCRIPTION: REAL ESTATE COMPANY/IMMOBILIENGESELLSCHAFT/SOCIÉTÉ IMMO-BILIERE ■ **3.** CLIENT: UPTOWN DESIGN FIRM: SULLIVAN PERKINS ART DIRECTOR: RON SULLIVAN DESIGNER: LINDA HELTON ILLUSTRATOR: DIANA MCKNIGHT DESCRIPTION: FOR A REAL ESTATE DEVEL-OPER /FÜR EIN IMMOBILIEN-GENERALUN-TERNEHMEN/POUR UN PROMOTEUR IMMOBILIER (USA) ■ **4.** CLIENT: J. RICHARD HILL & COMPANY DEVELOPERS DESIGN FIRM: RICHARDS BROCK MILLER MITCHELL & ASSOC. ART DIRECTOR/DESIGNER: D. C. STIPP DESCRIPTION: FOR A REAL ESTATE DEVELOPER /FÜR EIN IMMOBILIEN-GENERALUNTERNEHMEN/POUR UN PROMOTEUR IMMOBILIER (USA)

2

3

4

1

■ 1. CLIENT: BLACK DOG LAND COMPANY DESIGN FIRM: TOM SCHIFANELLA/ROBIN SHEPHERD STUDIOS ART DIRECTORS: TOM SCHIFANELLA/ROBIN SHEPHERD DESIGNER: TOM SCHIFANELLA ILLUSTRATORS: BOB COOPER/MIKE BARNHART DESCRIPTION: REAL ESTATE COMPANY/IMMOBILIENGESELLSCHAFT/SOCIÉTÉ IMMOBILIERE (USA)

INDUSTRY

INDUSTRIE

INDUSTRIES

■ **1.** Client: FOX RIVER PAPER COMPANY Design Firm: PENTAGRAM DESIGN Art Director/Designer: WOODY PIRTLE

1

■ **1.** Client: FOX RIVER PAPER COMPANY Design Firm: PENTAGRAM DESIGN Art Director/Designer: WOODY PIRTLE
Description: FOR A PAPER COMPANY/FÜR EINEN PAPIERHERSTELLOR/POUR UN FABRICANT DE PAPIER (USA)

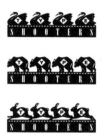

■ **1.** Client: PEGASUS PRINT AND DISPLAY Design Firm: KB DESIGN Art Directors: KAREN BLINCOES /RICHARD FISHER-SMITH Illustrator: RICHARD FISHER-SMITH Description: FOR A PRINTER; A VISUAL ALLUSION TO THE CLIENT'S NAME/FÜR EINEN DRUCKER; EINE ANSPIELUNG AUF DEN NAMEN DES KUNDEN/POUR UN IMPRIMEUR; ALLUSION AU NOM DU CLIENT (GBR) ■ **2.** Client: PRINTCRAFT, INC. Design Firm: CHARLES S. ANDERSON DESIGN CO Art Directors/Designers: CHARLES S. ANDERSON/DAN OLSON Illustrators: CHARLES S. ANDERSON/DAN OLSON/RANDY DAHLK Description: FOR A PRINTING COMPANY/FÜR EINE DRUCKEREI/POUR UNE IMPRIMERIE (USA) ■ **3.** Client: TYPE SHOOTERS Design Studio: THE DUFFY DESIGN GROUP Art Director/Designer: SARA LEDGARD Illustrators: SARA LEDGARD/LYNN SCHLUTE Description: FOR A TYPESETTER; A VISUAL PUN ON THE CLIENT'S NAME/FÜR EINE SETZEREI; EINE ANSPIELUNG AUF DEN NAMEN DES KUNDEN: "SATZ-SCHÜTZEN"/POUR UN ATELIER DE COMPOSITION; LES TIREURS FONT ALLUSION AU NOM DU CLIENT (USA)

4

5

6

■ **5.** Client: PANTONE Design Firm: CHARLES S. ANDERSON DESIGN CO. Art Directors/Designers: CHARLES S. ANDERSON/DAN OLSON Description: PROPOSED LOGO FOR A MANUFACTURER OF PAPER, PRINTING INKS, AND A COLOR MATCHING SYSTEM/LOGO-ENTWURF FÜR EINEN HERSTELLER VON PAPIER, DRUCKFARBEN UN FARBABSTIMM-SYSTEMEN/PROJET DE LOGO POUR UN FABRICANT DE PAPI-ER, D'ENCRES D'IMPRESSION ET D'UN SYSTÉME D'HARMONISATION DES COULEURS (USA) ■ **6.** Client: REARDON & KREBS, INC. Design Firm: PAUL CURTIN DESIGN Art Director: PAUL CURTIN Designer: ROBIN TERRA Description: FOR A TYPOGRAPHER/FÜR EINE SETZEREI/POUR UN TYPOGRAPHE (USA) ■ **7.** Client: MAS PRINTING CO. Art Director: BÜLENT ERKMEN Designer: BÜLENT ERKMEN Description: FOR A PRINTING COMPANY/FÜR EINE DRUCKEREI/POUR UNE IMPRIMERIE (TUR)

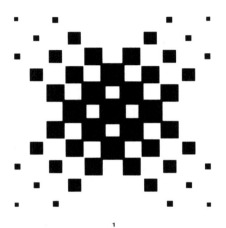

1

■ 1. CLIENT: CROSSPOINT SEMICONDUCTOR DESIGN FIRM: PAUL CURTIN DESIGN ART DIRECTOR: PAUL CURTIN DESIGNER: PETER LOCKE DESCRIPTION: FOR A MANUFACTURER OF SEMICONDUCTORS/FÜR EINEN HERSTELLER VON HALBLEITERN/POUR UN FABRICANT DE SEMICONDUCTEURS (USA) ■ 2. CLIENT: CANUS PLASTICS INC. DESIGN FIRM: NEVILLE SMITH GRAPHIC DESIGN ART DIRECTOR/DESIGNER: NEVILLE SMITH DESCRIPTION: FOR A PLASTICS MANUFACTURER/FÜR EINEN PLASTIKHERSTELLER/POUR UN FABRICANT DE MATIERES PLASTIQUES (CAN) ■ 3. CLIENT: METROCEL DESIGN FIRM: RICHARDS BROCK MILLER MITCHELL & ASSOC. ART DIRECTOR/DESIGNER: STEVE MILLER DESCRIPTION: FOR A CEL-LULAR TELEPHONE COMPANY/FÜR EINEN HERSTELLER VON MOBIL-TELEPHONEN/POUR UNE ENTREPRISE DE TÉLÉPHONES MOBILES (USA) ■ 4. CLIENT: MAILMATE DESIGN FIRM: SMIT GHORMLEY SANFT DESIGN ART DIRECTOR/DESIGNER: BRAD GHORMLEY DESCRIPTION: FOR A MAILING LIST SOFTWARE COMPANY/FÜR EINEN HERSTELLER VON SOFTWARE FÜR ADRESSENVERWALTUNG/POUR UN SOCIÉTÉ DE LOGICIELS DE PUBLIPOSTAGE ■ 5. CLIENT: LARSON FLAG POLES DESIGN FIRM: COLLISON DESIGN DESIGNER: LEE COLLISON DESCRIPTION: FOR A MANUFACTURER OF FLAGPOLES/FÜR EINEN HERSTELLER VON FAHNENSTANGEN/POUR UN FABRICANT DE MATS À DRAPEAUX (USA) ■ 6. CLIENT: CANADA SYSTEMS GROUP DESIGN FIRM: RAYMOND LEE & ASSOCIATES, LTD. ART DIRECTOR/DESIGNER: RAYMOND LEE ILLUSTRATOR: PETER BAKER DESCRIPTION: FOR A COMPUTER SOFTWARE COMPANY/FÜR EINEN HERSTELLER VON COMPUTER-SOFTWARE/POUR UN FABRICANT DE LOGICIELS (CAN) ■ 7. CLIENT: ORYX ENERGY DESIGN FIRM: RICHARDS BROCK MILLER MITCHELL & ASSOC. ART DIRECTOR/DESIGNER: STEVE MILLER DESCRIPTION: FOR AN ENERGY COMPANY; THE LOGO ALLUDES TO THE ORYX, THE ANIMAL FOR WHICH THE COMPANY IS NAMED/FÜR EINE ENERGIE-GESELLSCHAFT; THEMA DES LOGOS IST EINES ANTILOPENART, NACH DER DIE FIRMA GENANNT IST/POUR UN PRODUCTEUR D'ÉNERGIE; LE LOGO SE RAPPORTE À L'ANTILOPE QUI A DONNÉ SON NOM À L'ENTREPRISE (USA)

2

3

4

5

6

7

1

2

3

4

■ **1.** Client: OLSON GASKET COMPANY Design Firm: COLLISON DESIGN Designer: LEE COLLISON Description: FOR A MANUFACTURER OF GASKETS/FÜR EINEN HERSTELLER VON DICHTUNGEN/POUR UN FABRICANT DE JOINTS D'ÉTANCHÉITÉ (USA) ■ **2.** Client: H. LUKENS CONSTRUCTION COMPANY Design Firm: SMIT GHORMLEY SANFT DESIGN Art Director/Designer: BRAD GHORMLEY Description: FOR A CONSTRUCTION COMPANY/FÜR EINE BAUFIRMA/POUR UNE ENTREPRISE DES CONSTRUCTION (USA) ■ **3.** Client: TRAVIS CONSTRUCTION Design Firm: PENTAGRAM DESIGN Art Director/Designer: WOODY PIRTLE Description: FOR A CONSTRUCTION COMPANY/FÜR EINE BAUFIRMA/POUR UNE ENTREPRISE DE CONSTRUCTION (USA) ■ **4.** Client: WALL DATA Design Firm: TIM GIRVIN Art Director/Designer /Illustrator: TIM GIRVIN Description: THE IMAGE PORTRAYS THE PARTNERSHIP BETWEEN THE PC AND THE MAINFRAME COMPUTER/FÜR EINE COMPUTERFIRMA; DARGESTELLT IST DIE PARTNER-SCHAFT ZWISCHEN PC UND EINEM GROSSRECHENSYSTEM/LOGO D'UNE FIRME D'ORDINATEURS; L'IMAGE SYMBOLISE L'ASSOCIATION ENTRE ORDINATEUR INDIVIDUEL ET SYSTEMS CENTRAUX (USA)

1

2

3

■ **1.** CLIENT: CORNING INCORPORATED DESIGN FIRM: CORNING CORPORATE DESIGN DESIGNER /ILLUSTRATOR: DOUGLAS G. HARP DESCRIPTION: FOR A GLASS MANUFACTURER; THE "Q," EXTENDED INTO THE SHAPE OF AN APPLE, IS THE COMPANY'S SYMBOL FOR ITS "TOTAL QUALITY SYSTEM"/FÜR EINEN GLASHERSTELLER' DAS 'Q', DAS ZU EINEM APFEL WIRD, STECHT FÜR DAS "QUALITÄTS-SYSTEM" DER FIRMA/POUR UN FABRICANT DE VERRE; LE 'Q' EN FORME DE POMME SYMBOLISE LE LABEL DE QUALITÉ DE L'ENTREPRISE (USA) ■ **2.** CLIENT: INGRAM ASPHALT CO DESIGN FIRM: COLLISON DESIGN ART DIRECTOR/DESIGNER: LEE COLLISON DESCRIPTION: FOR A PAVING COMPANY/FÜR EINE STRASSENBAUFIRMA/ENTREPRISE DE REVÊTEMENTS DE ROUTES ■ **3.** CLIENT: ALPINE COOL DESIGN FIRM: FORMAZ ART DIRECTOR/ DESIGNER/ILLUSTRATOR: CLANE GRAVES DESCRIPTION: FOR A NOVELTY MANUFACTURER/FÜR EINEN HERSTELLER VON SCHIEBETÜREN UND TRENNWÄNDER/POUR UN PRODUCTEUR DE VERRE ET DE MIROIRS (USA)

4

5

6

■ **4.** Client: DARBIRAN CO., LTD. Design Firm: NESHANEH ART & DESIGN CO., LTD. Art Director/ Designer: IRAJ MIRZA-ALIKHANI Description: FOR A PRODUCER OF GLASS AND MIRRORS/FÜR EINEN HERSTELLER VON GLAS UND SPIEGELN/POUR UN PRODUCTEUR DE VERRE ET DE MIROIRS (IRN) ■ **5.** Client: MORS Design Firm: SAMENWEKENDE ONTWERPERS Art Director/Designer: ANDRÉ TOET Description: FOR A CEILING CONSTRUCTION COMPANY/FÜR EINE AUF ZIMMERDECKEN SPEZIALI-SIORTE BAUFIRMA/POUR UN CONSTRUCTEUR DE PLAFONDS (NLD) ■ **6.** Client: BELDAN LTD Design Firm: KB DESIGN Art Director: KAREN BLINCOE Designer: VANESSA RYAN Description: FOR A COMPA-NY THAT PRODUCES SLIDING DOORS AND PARTITIONS/FÜR EINEN HERSTELLER VON SCHIEBETÜREN UN TRENNWÄNDEN/POUR UNE ENTREPRISE FABRIQUANT DES PORTES COULISSANTES ET DES CLOISONS (GBR)

1

■ 1. Client: ALTUS COMMUNICATIONS, INC. Design Firm: SULLIVAN PERKINS Art Director: RON SULLIVAN Designer: JON FLAMING Description: FOR A TELECOMMUNICATIONS COMPANY/FÜR EINE TELEKOMMUNIKATIONSFIRMA/POUR UNE SOCIÉTÉ DE TÉLÉCOMMUNICATIONS (USA) ■ 2. Client: MR. MAILBOX Design Firm: GIBBS DESIGN, INC. Art Director/Designer: STEVE GIBBS Description: FOR A DESIGNER OF LETTER-BOXES/FÜR EINEN DESIGNER/INSTALLATEUR VON BRIEFKÄSTEN/POUR UN CONCEPTEUR DE BOITES À LETTRES (USA) ■ 3. Client: THE GUTTMAN GROUP Design Firm: AGNEW MOYER SMITH INC. Art Director/Designer: DON MOYER Description: FOR A CONGLOMERATE MADE UP OF FOUR COMPANIES/FÜR EIN KONGLOMERAT, DAS AUS VIER FIRMEN BESTCHT/POUR UN CONGLOMÉRAT FORMÉ PAR QUATRE ENTREPRISES (USA) ■ 4. Client: DENNISON STATIONERY PRODUCTS Design Firm: CROCKER INC. Art Director/Designer: BRUCE CROCKER Illustrator: MARK FISHER Description: AN IDENTITY TO REFLECT THE STATIC CLING PROPERTIES OF THE PRODUCT'S MATERIAL/LOGO ZUR SPIEGELUNG DES HAFTVERMEGENS DES FÜR DAS PRODUCKT VERWENDETEN MATERIALS/LOGO REFLÉTANT LES PROPRIÉTÉS ADHÉSIVES DU MATÉRIEL DONT EST FAIT LE PRODUIT ■ 5. Client: PORT AUTHORITY OF ALLEGHENY COUNTY Design Firm: AGNEW MOYER SMITH, INC. Art Directors: AGNEW MOYER SMITH, INC. Designer: DON MOYER Description: FOR A NEW LIGHT-RAIL PUBLIC TRANSPORTATION SYSTEM IN PITTSBURGH, CALLED THE "T"/FÜR EINEN NEUES ÖFFENTLICHES SCHIENEN-TRANSPORT-MITTEL IN PITTSBURGH, "T" GENANNT/POUR UN NOUVEAU SYSTEME ULTRALÉGER DE TRANSPORT SUR RAIL À PITTSBURGH CONNU SOUS LE NOM DE TRAIN T (USA) ■ 6. Client: HEBER BINARY PROJECT Design Firm: STEFANKO & HETZ ADVERTISING & DESIGN Art Director/Designer: MICHAEL HETZ Illustrator: JOANN HEALLY Description: FOR A GEOTHERMAL PLANT/FÜR EIN GEOTHERMISCHES KRAFTWERK/POUR UNE CENTRALE GÉOTHERMIQUE (USA)

2

3

STATIC IMAGES™

4

5

6

■ 1. CLIENT: OXO INTERNATIONAL PROJECT MANAGER: DAVIN STOWELL DESIGNER: RIE NØRREGAARD DESCRIPTION:

1

■ 1. CLIENT: OXO INTERNATIONAL PROJECT MANAGER: DAVIN STOWELL DESIGNER: RIE NØRREGAARD DESCRIPTION: FOR A MANUFACTURERS OF KITCHEN IMPLEMENTS/FÜR EINEN HERSTELLER VON KÜCHENGERÄTEN/POUR UN PRODUCTEURS D'AGENCEMETS DE CUISINES (USA)

CULINARY

KULINARISCH

CULINAIRE

1

■ 1. CLIENT: CHOCOLATE WORKS, HARBOURSIDE DESIGN FIRM: ANNETTE HARCUS DESIGN ART DIRECTOR/DESIGNER: ANNETTE HARCUS DESCRIPTION: FOR A CONFECTIONER SPECIALIZING IN CHOCOLATE/FÜR EINEN AUF SCHOLKOADE SPEZIALISIERTEN SÜSSWARENHERSTELLER/POUR UN FABRICANT DE BONBONS AU CHOCOLAT (AUS)

1

2

3

4

5

6

■ **1.** Client: CHEF'S PRIDE Design Firm: TRADEMARK DESIGN LIMITED Art Director: CLIVE GAY Designer: HELENE SWART Description: FOR A POULTRY WHOLESALER/FÜR EINEN GEFLÜGEL-GROSSHÄNDLER/POUR UN NÉGOCIANT DE VOLAILLE EN GROS (GBR) ■ **2.** Client: WATERFRONT TAVERN/SANCTUARY COVE RESORT Design Firm: BARRIE TUCKER DESIGN PTY LTD Art Director: BARRIE TUCKER Designer: CAZ TILLY Description: FOR A TAVERN AT A RESORT COMPLEX/FÜR EIN LOKAL IN EINEM FERIENORT/POUR UN CAFÉ-RESTAURANT DANS UN SITE TOURISTIQUE (AUS) ■ **3.** Client: AMAZON CLUB Design Firm: GIBBS DESIGN Art Director/Designer: STEVE GIBBS Description: FOR A "TROPICAL" CLUB IN A COLORADO SKI-RESORT TOWN/FÜR EINEN "TROPEN-CLUB" IN EINEM WINTERSPORTORT IN COLORADO/POUR UN CLUB "DES TROPIQUES" DANS UNE STATION DE SPORTS D'HIVER DU COLORADO (USA) ■ **4.** Client: BROOKLYN BREWERY Design Firm: MILTON GLASER, INC. Art Director/Designer: MILTON GLASER Description: FOR A BREWERY/FÜR EINE BRAUEREI/POUR UNE BASSERIE (USA) ■ **5.** Client: ONE SMART COOKIE Design Firm: SULLIVAN PERKINS Art Director: RON SULLIVAN Designer: DIANA MCKNIGHT Description: FOR A BAKERY SPECIALIZING IN COOKIES/FÜR EINE AUF KEKSO SPEZIALISIERTE BÄCKEREI/POUR UNE BOULANGERIE SPÉCIALISÉE DANS LE BISCUIT (USA) ■ **6.** Client: APPLE COMPUTER, INC. Design Firm: PROFILE DESIGN Art Director: THOMAS MCNULTY Designers: RUSSELL BAKER/KENICHI NISHIWAKI Description: FOR A CAFETERIA SERVING ONLY APPLE EMPLOYEES/FÜR EINE CAFETERIA DIE DEN ANGESTELLTEN VON APPLE VORBEHALTEN IST/POUR UNE CAFÉTÉRIA RÉSERVÉE AUX EMPLOYÉS D'APPLE (USA)

1

2

3

■ 1. CLIENT: THE BLUE FOX RESTAURANT DESIGN FIRM: MELANIE DOHERTY DESIGN ART DIRECTOR: MELANIE DOHERTY DESIGNERS: MELANIE DOHERTY/CHRISTINA DONNA (USA) ■ 2. CLIENT: HOG HEAVEN DESIGN FIRM: ANNETTE HARCUS DESIGN PTY LTD ART DIRECTOR/DESIGNER/ILLUSTRATOR: ANNETTE HARCUS (AUS) ■ 3. CLIENT: CITYBLOCK RESTAURANT DESIGN FIRM: WILLIAM REUTER DESIGN ART DIRECTOR/DESIGNER: WILLIAM REUTER DESCRIPTION: FOR A RESTAURANT; THE LOGO DESIGN ECHOES THE FAÇADE OF THE BUILDING/FÜR EINE RESTAURANT; IM LOGO WIEDERHOLT SICH DIE FASSADE DES GEBÜADES/POUR UN RESTAURANT; LE LOGO REPREND LES ÉLÉMENTS DE FAÇADE (USA)

4

5

6

■ **4.** CLIENT: FOUR-IN-HAND BAR AND RESTAURANT DESIGN FIRM: ANNETTE HARCUS DESIGN PTY LTD ART DIRECTORS: ANNETTE HARCUS/TREVOR CRUMP DESIGNER/ILLUSTRATOR: ANNETTE HARCUS (AUS) ■ **5.** CLIENT: BEDFORD PROPERTIES DESIGN FIRM: VANDERBYL DESIGN ART DIRECTOR /DESIGNER: MICHAEL VANDERBYL DESCRIPTION: FOR A RESTAURANT NAMED "LASCAUX"/FÜR EIN RESTAURANT MIT DEM NAMEN "LASCAUX"/POUR UN RESTAURANT BAPTISÉ "LASCAUX" (USA) ■ **6.** USA CLIENT: EMBARKO DESIGN FIRM: BLACKDOG DESIGNER/ILLUSTRATOR: MARK FOX DESCRIPTION: FOR A NEW RESTAURANT ON THE EMBARCADERO/ALS BILDERRÄTSEL GESTALTETES LOGO FÜR EIN NEUE RESTAURANT/LOGO EN FORME DE RÉBUS POUR UN NOUVEAU RESTAURANT (USA)

Pane e Vino

TRATTORIA

1

■ 1. CLIENT: PANE E VINO DESIGN FIRM: ROD DYER GROUP DESIGNER: BILL MURPHY (USA) ■ 2. CLIENT: THE 26TH STREET GRILL/COLORADO PLACE DESIGN FIRM: THE ROD DYER GROUP ART DIRECTOR: ROD DYER DESIGNER: BILL MURPHY (USA) ■ 3. CLIENT: TULIPE RESTAURANT DESIGN FIRM: ROD DYER GROUP DESIGNER: HARRIET BREITBORDE (USA) ■ 4. CLIENT: BIX RESTAURANT LOUNGE DESIGN FIRM: ROD DYER GROUP ART DIRECTOR: ROD DYER DESIGNER: CLIVE PERCY (USA) ■ 5. CLIENT: VICTOR HUGO'S DESIGN FIRM: ROD DYER GROUP DESIGNER: HARRIET BREITBORDE (USA)

2

3

4

5

1

■ 1. CLIENT: MORAY'S/CATAMARAN RESORT HOTEL DESIGN FIRM: DAVID CARTER GRAPHIC DESIGN ASSOCIATES CREATIVE DIRECTOR: DAVID CARTER ART DIRECTOR/DESIGNER: GARY LOBUE, JR. DESCRIPTION: RESTAURANT AT A RESORT HOTEL/RESTAURANT IN EINEM FERIENHOTEL/RESTAURANT D'UN HOTEL DE VACANCES (USA)

RETAIL   ·

EINZELHANDEL

VENTE AU DÉTAIL

1

■ 1. Client: MESA RETAIL STORE Design Firm: SIBLEY/PETEET DESIGN Art Director/Designer: REX
PETEET Description: FOR A STORE SPECIALIZING IN SOUTHWESTERN ITEMS/FÜR EINEN LADEN, DER SICH
AUF MÖBEL UND KUNSTHANDWERK AUS DEM SÜDWESTEN DER USA SPEZIALISIERT HAT/LOGO D'UN MAGA-
SIN SPÉCIALISÉ DANS LA VENTE DE MEUBLES ET D'ARTISANAT DU DUD-OUEST DE ETATS-UNIS (USA)

1

2

3

4

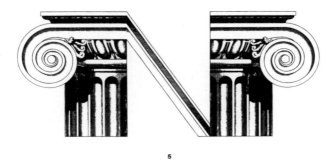

5

■ **1.** CLIENT: NATURAL ORGANICS INC. DESIGN FIRM: SHAPIRO DESIGN ASSOCIATES INC ART DIRECTOR/DESIGNER: ELLEN SHAPIRO DESCRIPTION: FOR A "HOLISTIC" RETAIL STORE SELLING NATURAL FOODS, VITAMINS, BOOKS, AND SO FORTH/FÜR EINEN "ALTERNATIV"-LADEN, IN DEM NAURPRODUKTE, VITAMINPRÄPARATE, BÜCHER UND SO WEITER VERKAUFT WERDEN/POUR UNE BOUTIQUE ALTERNATIVE OU L'ON TROUVE DES PRODUITS NATURELS, DES VITAMINES, DES LEVRES, ETC. (USA) ■ **2.** CLIENT: SHAVANO PARK/MELVIN SIMON & ASSOC. DESIGN FIRM: SIBLEY/PETEET DESIGN ART DIRECTOR/DESIGNER: REX PETEET DESCRIPTION: FOR A SHOPPING CENTER IN WOODED AREA OUTSIDE SAN ANTONIO, TEXAS/FÜR EIN EINKAUFSZENTRUM IN EINER BEWALDETEN GEGEND AUSSERHALB VON SAN ANTONIO, TEXAS/POUR UN CENTRE COMMERICAL DANS UNE RÉGION BOISÉE PRES DE SAN ANTONIO, TEXAS (USA) ■ **3.** CLIENT: GARDINE DESIGN FIRM: JÜRGEN FÖRSTER ART DIRECTOR/DESIGNER: JÜRGEN FÖRSTER DESCRIPTION: FOR A BOUTIQUE SPECIALIZING IN CURTAINS/FÜR EINE AUF VORHÄNGE SPEZIALISIERTE BOUTIQUE/POUR UNE BOUTIQUE DE DÉCORATION RIDEAUX (GER) ■ **4.** CLIENT: TOKYO PRÉT-A-PORTER DESIGN FIRM: IGARASHI STUDIO ART DIRECTOR: TAKENOBU IGARASHI DESIGNER: YUKIMI SASAGO DESCRIPTION: FOR A SPECIALTY STORE; THE LOGO IS MADE UP OF THE CHINESE CHARACTERS FOR "TOKYO"/FÜR EIN SPEZIA-LITÄTENGESCHÄFT; DIE BASIS DES LOGOS IST DAS CHINESISCHE SCHRIFTZEICHEN FÜR "TOKIO"/POUR UN MAGASIN DE SPÉCIALITÉS; LE LOGO EST COMPOSÉ DES CARACTERES CHINOIS POUR TOKYO (JPN) ■ **5.** CLIENT: NOVARA HOLDINGS INCORPORATED DESIGN FIRM: NEVILLE SMITH GRAPHIC DESIGN ART DIRECTOR/DESIGNER: NEVILLE SMITH DESCRIPTION: FOR AN IMPORTER OF ITALIAN GOODS /FÜR EINEN IMPORTEUR ITALIENISCHER WAREN/POUR UN IMPORTATEUR DE PRODUITS ITALIENS (CAN)

1

2

3

4

5

6

7

8

■ 1-16. CLIENT: BLOOMINGDALE'S ART DIRECTOR: ROBERT VALENTINE DESIGNER/ILLUSTRATOR: STEVEN SIKORA
DESCRIPTION: ILLUSTRATIONS REPRESENTING THE 12 CALIFORNIAS USED IN A STORE-WIDE CAMPAIGN BY
BLOOMINGDALE'S IN THE SPRING OF 1989 FOR THE STORE DIRECTORY, MENUS, DEPARTMENT AND PROD-
UCT PROMOTION, WINDOW AND AISLE DISPLAYS/ZWÖLF ZONEN KALIFORNIENS SIND HIER SYMBOLISIERT.

9

10

11

12

13

14

15

16

DIE ZEICHEN WURDEN VON BLOOMINGDALE'S IN EINER FRÜHJAHRSKAMPAGNE FÜR DIE LADENINFOR-
MATION, SPEISEKARTEN, WERBUNG, SCHAUFENSTER UND GESTELL-DISPLAYS VERWENDET/CES ILLUS-
TRATIONS SYMBOLISENT LES 12 PROVINCES DE LA CALIFORNIE. LES GRANDES MAGASINS BLOOMING-
DALE'S LES ONT UTILISÉES PARTOUT, SUR LES MENUS, LES PRÉSENTOIRES, SUR LES VITRINES, ETC. (USA)

1

musée

2

3

4

■ **1.** CLIENT: VIDEO CENTRAL DESIGN FIRM: RICHARDS BROCK MILLER MITCHELL & ASSOC. ART DIRECTOR/DESIGNER: KEN SHAFER DESCRIPTION: FOR A VIDEO OUTLET/FÜR EINE VIDEOTHEK/POUR UNE VIDÉOTHEQUE (USA) ■ **2.** CLIENT: MUSÉE INTERNATIONALE CO., LTD. DESIGN FIRM: IGARASHI STUDIO ART DIRECTOR: TAKENOBU IGARASHI DESIGNER: ROSS MC BRIDE DESCRIPTION: FOR AN IMPORTER AND RETAILER/FÜR EIN IMPORT- UND EINZELHANDELSGESCHÄFT/POUR UN CENTRE COMMERCIAL DOTÉ D'UN CAFÉ (JPN) ■ **3.** CLIENT: J. RICHARD HILL/CITY FAIR DESIGN FIRM: RICHARDS BROCK MILLER MITCHELL & ASSOC. ART DIRECTOR/DESIGNER: STEVE MILLER DESCRIPTION: LOGO REFLECTS THE ARCHITECTURAL DETAILS OF A SHOPPING CENTER/DAS LOGO BASIERT AUF ARCHITEKTONIS-CHEN DETAILS EINES BINKAUFSZENTRUMS/LOGO REFLÉTANT L'ARCHITECTURE D'UNE CENTRE COMMERCIAL (USA) ■ **4.** CLIENT: CLAYTRADE DESIGN FIRM: PRINCIPIA GRAPHICA ART DIRECTORS: ROBIN RICKABAUGH/HEIDI RICKABAUGH DESIGNERS: PAUL MORT/ROBIN RICKABAUGH DESCRIPTION: FOR A GIFT STORE SPECIALIZING IN CERAMICS/FÜR EINEN AUF KERAMIK SPEZIALISIERTEN LADEN FÜR GESCHENKARTIKEL/POUR UNE BOUTIQUE CADEAUX SPÉCIALISÉ DANS LA CÉRAMIQUE (USA)

1

■ 1. CLIENT: CITYBOOKS DESIGN FIRM: KIKU OBATA & COMPANY ART DIRECTOR: KIKU OBATA DESIGNER:
RICHARD NELSON DESCRIPTION: FOR A BOOKSTORE/FÜR EINEN BUCHLADEN/POUR UNE LIBRAIRIE (USA)

FASHION

MODE

MODE

1

■ **1.** Client: ROBERT BRUCE SWEATERS Design Firm: MICHAEL SCHWAB DESIGN Art Director: MICHAEL TOTH Designer/Illustrator: MICHAEL SCHWAB Description: DESIGNERS AND MANUFACTURERS OF SWEATERS/DESIGNER UND HERSTELLER VON PULLOVERN/CRÉATEURS ET FABRICANTS DE PULLOVERS (USA)

1

interwol

2

3

■ **1.** Cʟɪᴇɴᴛ: TOKIO LINGERIE Dᴇsɪɢɴ Fɪʀᴍ: PATTI NUNEZ Aʀᴛ Dɪʀᴇᴄᴛᴏʀ/Dᴇsɪɢɴᴇʀ/Iʟʟᴜsᴛʀᴀᴛᴏʀ: PATTI NUNEZ Dᴇsᴄʀɪᴘᴛɪᴏɴ: FOR A LINGERIE RETAILER/LOGO FÜR DAMENUNTERWÄSCHE/POUR DE LA LINGERIE FÉMININE (USA) ■ Cʟɪᴇ'ɴᴛ: INTERWOL Dᴇsɪɢɴ Fɪʀᴍ: JOLANTA CYLWIK-CHICTOWSKA Aʀᴛ Dɪʀᴇᴄᴛᴏʀ/Dᴇsɪɢɴᴇʀ: JOLANTA CYLWIK-CHICTOWSKA (POL) ■ **3.** Cʟɪᴇɴᴛ: SADAF JEWELRY Aʀᴛ Dɪʀᴇᴄᴛᴏʀ/Dᴇsɪɢɴᴇʀ: IRAJ MIRZA-ALIKHANI Dᴇsᴄʀɪᴘᴛɪᴏɴ: FOR A JEWELRY STORE; SADAF MEANS SHELL IN THE IRANIAN LANGUAGE/FÜR EINEN SCHMUCKLADEN; SADAF IST DAS IRANISCHE WORT FÜR MUSCHEL/POUR UNE BIJOUTERIE; "SADAF" EST LE COQUILLAGE EN IRANIEN (IRN)

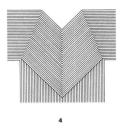

4

5

6

■ **4.** Cʟɪᴇɴᴛ: VT FASHION STUDIO Dᴇsɪɢɴ Fɪʀᴍ: DESIGNERS EXPRESS Aʀᴛ Dɪʀᴇᴄᴛᴏʀ/Dᴇsɪɢɴᴇʀ: BEN LAI Dᴇsᴄʀɪᴘᴛɪᴏɴ: FOR A TEE-SHIRT MANUFACTURER/FÜR EINEN HERSTELLER VON TEE-SHIRTS/POUR UN FABRICANT DE T-SHIRTS (USA) ■ **5.** Cʟɪᴇɴᴛ: EMPORIO HOMNIBUS RIMINI Aʀᴛ Dɪʀᴇᴄᴛᴏʀ/Dᴇsɪɢɴᴇʀ: MASSIMO DOLCINI (ITA) ■ **6.** Cʟɪᴇɴᴛ: ULRIKE ECKER Dᴇsɪɢɴ Fɪʀᴍ: STADLER & SUTER Aʀᴛ Dɪʀᴇᴄᴛᴏʀ/Dᴇsɪɢɴᴇʀ: BEAT KEUSCH Dᴇsᴄʀɪᴘᴛɪᴏɴ: FOR A SEAMSTRESS/DESIGNER /FÜR EINE SCHNEIDERIN/MODE-DESIGNERIN/POUR UNE COUTURIERE STYLICIENNE (SWI)

1

2

3

4

■ 1. CLIENT: KIRPI AGENCY: REKLAMEVI YOUNG & RUBICAM ART DIRECTOR/DESIGNER: BÜLENT ERKMEN
DESCRIPTION: FOR A SPORTSWEAR SHOP; KIRPI IS TURKISH FOR PORCUPINE/FÜR EINEN
SPORTBEKLEIDUNGSLADEN; KIRPI IST TÜRKISCH FÜR STACHELSCHWEIN/UN MAGASIN DE SPORT;
"KIRPI" EST LE PORC-ÉPIC EN TURC (TUR) ■ 2. CLIENT: YOUNG SONG APPAREL DESIGN FIRM:
BRUCE YELASKA DESIGN ART DIRECTOR/DESIGNER: BRUCE YELASKA DESCRIPTION: FOR A WOMEN'S
APPAREL COMPANY/FÜR EINE DAMENBEKLEIDUNGSFIRMA/POUR UNE ENTREPRISE DE TEXTILES
DAMES (USA) ■ 3. CLIENT: ALEXANDER JULIAN DESIGN FIRM: CHARLES S. ANDERSON DESIGN CO. ART
DIRECTOR/DESIGNER/ILLUSTRATOR: CHARLES S. ANDERSON DESCRIPTION: FOR THE DESIGNER'S CLOTH-
ING LINE FOR WOMEN/FÜR DIE DAMENMODE-LINIE DIESES DESIGNERS/POUR LES CRÉATIONS DE
MODE FÉMININE DE CE STYLICIEN (USA) ■ 4. CLIENT: SCHOOL PROJECT/CHAMELEON CLOTHING
ART DIRECTOR/DESIGNER: KEVIN M. LAUTERBACH DESCRIPTION: FOR A CLOTHING MANUFACTURER
/MARKENZEICHEN FÜR DIE TEXTILFIRMA CHAMELEON/MARQUE DES VETEMENTS CHAMELEON

1

■ 1. CLIENT: LEVI STRAUSS & CO DESIGN FIRM: ZIMMERMAN CROWE DESIGN ART DIRECTORS/DESIGNERS: DENNIS CROWE/NEAL ZIMMERMAN DESCRIPTION: MARK FOR CONTEMPORARY STRETCH JEANS PRODUCT APPEALING TO A YOUTHFUL MARKET/MARQUE D'IDENTIFICATION DES JEANS POUR LES JEUNE FILLES/JEANS-LINIE FÜR FRAUNEN (USA) ■ 2-5. CLIENT: LEE JEANS DESIGN FIRM: CHARLES S. ANDERSON DESIGN CO. ART DIRECTOR /DESIGNER/ILLUSTRATOR: CHARLES S. ANDERSON DESCRIPTION: PRODUCT IDENTITY FOR "BROKEN RULES" JEANS; THE NAME IS INSPIRED BY THE "GLAMOUR DON'TS" THE MAGAZINE'S FASHION TIPS; THE LOGOS ARE MEANT TO BE USED AS EMBROIDERED PATCHES ON JEANS/MARQUE D'IDENTIFICATION DES JEANS "BROKEN RULES"; LE NOM, "INFRACTION AUX REGLES," ETAIT ALLUSION AUX DIKTATS IMPOSÉS PAR LES MAGAZINES DE MODE; CE LOGO ORNE LES PANTALONS DE CETTE MARQUE (USA)

2

3

4

5

■ **1.** CLIENT: MODA HAIR DESIGN DESIGN FIRM: NEVILLE SMITH GRAPHIC DESIGN ART DIRECTOR

■ **1.** CLIENT: MODA HAIR DESIGN DESIGN FIRM: NEVILLE SMITH GRAPHIC DESIGN ART DIRECTOR
/DESIGNER/ILLUSTRATOR: NEVILLE SMITH DESCRIPTION: FOR A HAIR STYLIST/COIFFEUR/COIFFEUR (CAN)

CULTURAL

KULTUR

CULTURE

1

■ **1.** CLIENT: WYOMING COUNCIL OF THE ARTS DESIGN FIRM: BOB COONTS DESIGN GROUP ART DIRECTOR: BOB COONTS DESIGNER: GREG RATTENBURG DESCRIPTION: FOR THE WYOMING STATE ARTS ORGANIZATION IN THE AMERICAN WEST/FÜR EINE ÖFFENTLICHE KUNSTKOMMISSION IM AMERIKANISCHEN WESTON/POUR LA COMMISSION D'ART DE L'ETAT EN L'OUEST AMERICAIN (USA)

1

2

3

4

1

■ 1. CLIENT: NOPPON KAN HERITAGE ASSOCIATION DESIGN FIRM: YUTAKA K. SASAKI ART DIRECTOR/DESIGNER: YUTAKA K. SASAKI DESCRIPTION: FOR A PRODUCER OF CONCERTS OF TRADITIONAL AND MODERN JAPANESE MUSIC/FÜR EINEN KONZERTVERANSTALTER FÜR TRADITIONELLE UND MODERNE JAPANISCHE MUSIK/POUR UN ORGANISATEUR DE CONCERTS DE MUSIQUE JAPONAISE TRADITIONNELLE ET MODERNE (USA) ■ 2. CLIENT: DALLAS INSTITUTE OF VOCAL ARTS (DIVA) DESIGN FIRM: COLVIN RATTAN DESIGN ART DIRECTORS: ALAN COLVIN/JOE RATTAN DESCRIPTION: FOR A MUSIC SCHOOL/ FÜR EINE MUSIKAKADEMIE/POUR UNE ACADÉMIE DE MUSIQUE (USA) ■ 3. CLIENT: DALLAS REPERTORY THEATRE DESIGN FIRM: PETERSON & COMPANY ART DIRECTOR/DESIGNER: SCOTT RAY (USA) ■ 4. CLIENT: ACADEMIE DE MUSIQUE DESIGN FIRM: ALAIN ROCHON DESIGN ART DIRECTOR/DESIGNER: ALAIN ROCHON DESCRIPTION: FOR A MUSIC SERVICE ORGANIZATION/FÜR EINE MUSIKAKADEMIE/POUR UNE ACADÉMIE MUSIQUE (CAN) ■ 5. CLIENT: THE OPERA COMPANY OF DALLAS DESIGN FIRM: PENTAGRAM DESIGN ART DIRECTOR /DESIGNER: WOODY PIRTLE DESCRIPTION: FOR AN OPERA COMPANY/FÜR EIN OPERNHAUS/POUR UN OPÉRA (USA)

2

3

4

5

1

2

IDCNY

3

■ **1.** CLIENT: TURK EVI DESIGN FIRM: BÜLENT ERKMEN ART DIRECTOR/DESIGNER: BULENT ERKMEN DESCRIPTION: FOR A FOUNDATION INVOLVED IN ARCHITECTURAL CONSERVATION/FÜR EINE STIFTUNG FÜR DIE ERHALTUNG VON BAUDENKMÄLERN/POUR UNE FONDATION ŒUVRANT POUR LA PRESERVATION DU PATRIMOINE ARCHITECTURAL (TUR) ■ **2.** CLIENT: DALLAS HISTORICAL SOCIETY DESIGN FIRM: KNAPE & KNAPE ART DIRECTOR: WILLIE BARONET DESIGNER: MICHAEL CONNORS DESCRIPTION: PROPOSED LOGO FOR A HISTORICAL SOCIETY/LOGO-ENTWURF FÜR EINE HISTORISCHE GESELLSCHAFT/PROJET DE LOGO POUR UNE SOCIÉTÉ D'HISTOIRE (USA) ■ **3.** CLIENT: THE INTERNATIONAL DESIGN CENTER, NEW YORK DESIGN FIRM: VIGNELLI ASSOCIATES ART DIRECTOR/DESIGNER: MICHAEL BIERUT DESCRIPTION: A FURNISHINGS DESIGN RETAIL AND EXHIBITION CENTER/EIN VERKAUFS- UND AUSSTELLUNGSZENTRUM FÜR DESIGNER-BINRICHTUNG-SGEGEN-STÜNDE /CENTRE DE VENTE-EXPOSITION D'AMÉNAGEMENTS CONÇUS PAR DES STYLICIENS (USA)

4

5

6

■ **4.** CLIENT: PROMOTIVATORS DESIGN FIRM: RICHARDS BROCK MILLER MITCHELL & ASSOC. ART DIRECTOR/DESIGNER: DAVID BECK DESCRIPTION: FOR A GROUP OF "MOTIVATIONAL SPEAKERS"/FÜR EINE GRUPPE, DIE KADERIEUTE MOTIVIERT/POUR UN GROUPE DE CONFÉRENCIERS EXPERTS (USA) ■ **5.** CLIENT: STATE LIBRARY OF NEW SOUTH WALES DESIGN FIRM: SPATCHURST DESIGN ASSOCIATES PTY. LTD. ART DIRECTOR/DESIGNER: JOHN SPATCHURST DESCRIPTION: FOR A PUBLIC LIBRARY; THE LOGO IS INSPIRED BY THE "TREE OF KNOWLEDGE"/FÜR EINE ÖFFENTLICHE BIBLIOTHEK; DAS LOGO BASIERT AUF DEM "BAUM DER ERKENNTNIS"/POUR UNE BIBLIOTHEQUE PUBLIQUE; LE LOGO EST INSPIRÉ DE "L'ARBRE DE LA CONNAISSANCE" (AUS) ■ **6.** CLIENT: FRIENDS OF THE SAINT LOUIS PUBLIC LIBRARY DESIGN FIRM: KIKU OBATA & COMPANY ART DIRECTOR: KIKU OBATA DESIGNER: RICHARD NELSON DESCRIPTION: FOR A FUND-RAISING RUN FOR A PUBLIC LIBRARY/FÜR EINEN LAUF ZUGUNSTEN EINER ÖFFENTLICHEN BIBLIOTHEK/POUR UNE COURSE ORGANISÉE AU BÉNÉFICE D'UNE BIBLIOTHEQUE PUBLIQUE (USA)

1

2

■ **1.** CLIENT: AIGA MINNESOTA DESIGN FIRM: CHARLES S. ANDERSON DESIGN CO ART DIRECTOR: DAN OLSON DESIGNERS: DAN OLSON AND KOBE DESCRIPTION: FOR AN ANNUAL "DESIGN CAMP" IN THE WOODS OF NORTH-ERN MINNESOTA/FÜR EIN JÄHRLICH VERANSTALTETES "DESIGN-LAGER" IN DEN WÄLDERN DES NORDENS VON MINNESOTA/POUR UN "CAMP DE DESIGN" ANNUEL DAN LES FORETS DU NORD DU MINNESOTA (USA) ■ **2.** CLIENT: CITY OF PITTSBURGH DEPARTMENT OF PARKS AND RECREATION DESIGN FIRM: AGNEW MOYER SMITH INC. ART DIRECTOR/DESIGNER: REED AGNEW DESCRIPTION: FOR THE ZOO OF THE CITY OF PITTSBURGH/FÜR DEN STÄDTISCHEN ZOO VON PITTSBURGH/POUR LE ZOO DE LA VILLE DE PITTSBURGH (USA)

3

4

■ **3.** CLIENT: AMERICAN INSTITUTE OF GRAPHIC ARTISTS (AIGA) DESIGN FIRM: PETERSON & COMPANY ART DIRECTOR/DESIGNER: BRYAN L. PETERSON DESCRIPTION: SEVENTY-FIFTH ANNIVERSARY OF THE AIGA/FÜR DEN FÜNFUNDSIEBZIGSTEN GEBURTSTAG DES AIGA/75E ANNIVERSAIRE DE L'AIGA (USA) ■ **4.** CLIENT: THE DESIGN CONFERENCE THAT JUST HAPPENS TO BE IN PARK CITY(TDCTJHTBIPC) DESIGN FIRM: THE WELLER INSTITUTE FOR THE CURE OF DESIGN, INC. ART DIRECTOR/DESIGNER/ILLUSTRATOR: DON WELLER DESCRIPTION: DESIGN CONFERENCE IN A SKI RESORT TOWN/DESIGN-KONFERENZ IN EINEM WINTERSPORT-ORT/CONFÉRENCE DE DESIGN ORGANISÉE DANS UN STATION DE SPORTS D'HIVER (USA)

1

2

3

4

■ **1.** Client: OREGON STATE UNIVERSITY Design Firm: PRINCIPIA GRAPHICA Art Directors: ROBIN RICKABAUGH/DAVID HARDESTY/HEIDI RICKABAUGH/DON ROOD Designer: PAUL MORT Description: FOR A UNIVERSITY/FÜR EINE UNIVERSITÄT/POUR UNE UNIVERSITÉ (USA) ■ **2.** Client: NOVO DESIGN CENTER Design Firm: HEGSTROM DESIGN/KEOKI DESIGN Art Directors/Designers: KEN HAGSTROM/KEOKI WILLIAMS Description: FOR A DESIGN TRADE SCHOOL/FÜR EINE DESIGN-GACHSCHULE/POUR UNE ÉCOLE PROFESSIONNELLE DE DESIGN (USA) ■ **3.** Client: BUENA VISTA COLLEGE Design Firm: SAYLES GRAPHIC DESIGN Art Director/Designer: JOHN SAYLES Description: THE CENTENNNIAL LOGO FOR A COLLEGE/LOGO ZUN HUNDERTJAHRESFEIER EINES COLLEGE/LOGO POUR LE CENTENAIRE.D'UN COLLÉGE (USA) ■ **4.** Client: MINNEAPOLIS COLLEGE OF ART & DESIGN Design Firm: CHARLES S. ANDERSON DESIGN CO Art Directors: CHARLES S. ANDERSON/DAN OLSON Designers: CHARLES S. ANDERSON/DAN OLSON Illustrators: CHARLES S. ANDERSON/RANDY DAHLIK Description: FOR A COLLEGE OF DESIGN/FÜR EIN DESIGN-COLLEGE/POUR UN COLLEGE DE DESIGN (USA)

1

■ 1. Client: SOUTH AUSTRALIA SCHOOL OF DESIGN Design Firm: BARRIE TUCKER DESIGN PTY LTD Art Director: JODY TUCKER Designers: JODY TUCKER/JOHN ALLERT/NICHOLAS ELDRIDGE Description: 29 DEGREES, AN IDENTITY DESIGNED BY STUDENTS FOR A SERIES OF PROJECTS COMPLETED BY 29 GRADUATING STUDENTS/"29 DEGREES" DÉSIGNE UN PROGRAMME D'IDENTITÉ CONÇU PAR DES ÉTUDI- ANTS POUR UNE SÉRIE DE PROJETS QUI ONT ÉTÉ RÉALISÉS PAR 29 CANDIDATS AUX EXAMENS (AUS)

RECREATION

ERHOLUNG

LOISIRS

1

■ 1. CLIENT: VAGABOND SOCCER TEAM DESIGN FIRM: SULLIVAN PERKINS ART DIRECTOR: RON SULLIVAN DESIGNER: JON FLAMING DESCRIPTION: SOCCER TEAM/FÜR EINE FUSSBALLMANNSCHAFT/POUR UNE ÉQUIPE DE FOOTBALL (USA)

1

■ **1.** CLIENT: TEAM MAD DOG DESIGN FIRM: RICHARDS BROCK MILLER MITCHELL & ASSOC. ART DIRECTOR/ DESIGNER: KEN SHAFER DESCRIPTION: MOTORCYCLE RACING TEAM/MOTORRAD-RENNMANN-SCHAFT/ÉQUIPE DE COUREURS MOTOCYCLISTES (USA) ■ **2.** CLIENT: TGI FRIDAY'S DESIGN FIRM: RICHARDS BROCK MILLER MITCHELL & ASSOC. ART DIRECTOR/DESIGNER: KENNY GARRISON DESCRIPTION: "BARTENDERS' OLYMPICS" SPONSORED BY A RESTAURANT CHAIN/"OLYMPIADE DE BAR-MÄNNER", ORGANISIERT VON EINTER RESTAURANTKETTE/"JEUX OLYMPIQUES DES BARMEN" ORGAN-ISÉS PAR UNE CHAINE DE RESTAURANTS (USA) ■ **3.** CLIENT: SIRIUS FITNESS DESIGN FIRM: COLLISON DESIGN ART DIRECTOR/DESIGNER: LEE COLLISON DESCRIPTION: HEALTH CLUB/FITNESS-ZENTRUM/FIT-NESS-CLUB (USA) ■ **4.** CLIENT: SEGIVIA GOLF CLUB DESIGN FIRM: KAZUMASA NAGAI ART DIRECTOR/DESIGNER: KAZUMASA NAGAI DESCRIPTION: COUNTRY CLUB/COUNTRY CLUB/COUNTRY-CLUB (JPN)

2

SIRIUS FITNESS

3

4

1

2

3

4

5

■ **1.** CLIENT: CALHOUN BEACH CLUB DESIGN FIRM: THE DUFFY DESIGN GROUP ART DIRECTOR/DESIGNER/ ILLUSTRATOR: HALEY JOHNSON DESCRIPTION: FOR A WATER SPORTS CLUB/FÜR EINEN WASSERSPORT-CLUB/POUR UN CLUB DE SPORTS NAUTIQUES (USA) ■ **2.** CLIENT: FALLON MCELLIGOTT DESIGN FIRM: THE DUFFY DESIGN GROUP ART DIRECTOR/DESIGNER: JOE DUFFY ILLUSTRATORS: JOE DUFFY/LYNN SCHULTE DESCRIPTION: (2-4) LOGOS FOR AN ADVERTISING FIRM'S OWN ATHLETIC TEAMS/LOGOS FÜR DIE SPORT-TEAMS EINER WERBEAGENTUR/ LOGOS POUR LES ÉQUIPES SPORTIVES D'UNE AGENCE DE PUBLICITÉ (USA) ■ **3.** CLIENT: FALLON MCELLIGOTT DESIGN FIRM: THE DUFFY DESIGN GROUP ART DIRECTOR/DESIGNER: SARA LEDGARD ILLUSTRATORS: SARA LEDGARD/LYNN SCHULTE ■ **4.** CLIENT: FALLON MCELLIGOTT DESIGN FIRM: THE DUFFY DESIGN GROUP ART DIRECTOR/DESIGNER/ILLUSTRATOR: SARA LEDGARD (USA) ■ **5.** CLIENT: ROLEX DESIGN FIRM: THE DUFFY DESIGN GROUP ART DIRECTOR/DESIGNER: CHARLES S. ANDERSON ILLUSTRATORS: CHARLES S. ANDERSON/LYNN SCHULTE DESCRIPTION: PROPOSED SYMBOL FOR A COLLEGIATE TENNIS TOURNAMENT SPONSORED BY ROLEX/ENTWURF EINES SYMBOLS FÜR EIN COLLEGE-TENNISTOURNIER, DAS VON ROLEX VERANSTALTET WIRD/PROJET D'EMBLEME POUR UN TOURNOI DE TENNIS INTERCOLLEGES PARRAINÉ PAR ROLEX (USA)

1

2

■ **1.** CLIENT: TURKISH ARCHERY FEDERATION DESIGN FIRM: BÜLENT ERKMEN ART DIRECTOR/DESIGNER: BÜLENT ERKMEN DESCRIPTION: FOR AN ARCHERY ORGANIZATION/FÜR EINEN VERBAND DER BOGENSCHÜTZEN/POUR UNE ASSOCIATION DE TIREURS À L'ARC (TUR) ■ **2.** CLIENT: L. A. CHE-VAUCHÉE CO., LTD. DESIGN FIRM: MICHIO MIYABAYASHI ART DIRECTOR/DESIGNER: MICHIO MIYABAYASHI (JPN)

3

4

■ **3.** CLIENT: LOST PINES/BOY SCOUTS OF AMERICA DESIGN FIRM: COLLISON DESIGN DESIGNER: LEE COLLISON DESCRIPTION: LOGO FOR A BOY SCOUT SUMMER CAMP ■ **4.** CLIENT: BEDFORD PROPERTIES DESIGN FIRM: VANDERBYL DESIGN ART DIRECTOR/DESIGNER: MICHAEL VANDERBYL DESCRIPTION: FOR A RESORT DEVELOPMENT IN HAWAII THAT OVERLOOKS THE HISTORICAL FLOWER-GROWING REGION OFF THE ISLAND (USA)

1

2

3

■ **1.** CLIENT: PEBBLE BEACH COMPANY DESIGN FIRM: GENSLER AND ASSOCIATES/GRAPHICS ART DIRECTOR/DESIGNER: JOHN BRICKLER DESCRIPTION: RETAIL STORE AT A RESORT COMPLEX/LADEN IN EINEM FERIENORT/MAGASIN LOGÉ DANS UN COMPLEXE TOURISTIQUE (USA) ■ **2.** CLIENT: ESSEX & SUSSEX DESIGN FIRM: DUFFY DESIGN GROUP ART DIRECTOR/DESIGNER: CHARLES S. ANDERSON ILLUSTRATORS: CHARLES S. ANDERSON/LYNN SCHULTE DESCRIPTION: FOR A PAIR OF LUXURY HOTELS/FÜR DIE LUXUS-HOTELS ESSEX UND SUSSEX/LOGO DES HOTELS DE LUXE ESSEX ET SUSSEX (USA) ■ **3.** CLIENT: HILTON INTERNATIONAL CAIRNS DESIGN FIRM: BARRIE TUCKER DESIGN PTY LTD ART DIRECTORS: BARRIE TUCKER/ISOBELLE POVER DESIGNERS: BARRIE TUCKER/BRENTON HILL DESCRIPTION: HOTEL (AUS)

4

THE RESORT AT SQUAW CREEK

6

■ **4.** Client: THE SPA AT THE CRESCENT/ROSEWOOD HOTELS Design Firm: DAVID CARTER GRAPHIC DESIGN ASSOCIATES Creative Director: DAVID CARTER Art Director/Designer: GARY LOBUE, JR. Illustrator: JIM SWEENEY Description: SPA AND HEALTH CLUB AT A RESORT HOTEL/KUR- UND FITNESS- CLUB IN EINEM FERIENHOTEL/CLUB DE SOINS THERMAUX ET DE SANTÉ DANS UN HOTEL TOURISTIQUE (USA) ■ **5.** Client: HOTEL MYNDOS Design Firm: BÜLENT ERKMEN Art Director/Designer: BÜLENT ERKMEN Description: FOR A SUMMER RESORT HOTEL/FÜR EIN HOTEL AN EINEM SOMMERFERIENORT/HOTEL BAL- NÉAIRE (TUR) ■ **6.** Client: PERINI RESORTS, INC. Design Firm: MELANIE DOHERTY DESIGN Art Director/Designer: MELANIE DOHERTY Illustrator: ANTHONY RUSSO Description: RESORT AND CONFERENCE CENTER/FERIENORT UND KONGRESSZENTRUM/STATION TOURISTIQUE DOTÉE D'UN PALAIS DES CONGRES (USA)

Hamoa Beach Club

1

■ 1. CLIENT: HAMOA BEACH CLUB/ROSEWOOD HOTELS DESIGN FIRM: DAVID CARTER GRAPHIC DESIGN ASSOCIATES CREATIVE DIRECTOR: DAVID CARTER ART DIRECTOR/DESIGNER: GARY LOBUE, JR. ILLUSTRATOR: BYRON HAYNES DESCRIPTION: FOR A RESORT HOTEL/FÜR EIN HOTEL AN EINEM FERIENORT/POUR UN HOTEL TOURISTIQUE (USA)

VARIA

VARIA

VARIA

1

■ 1. CLIENT: HILDESHEIMER FORUM DESIGN FIRM: KOMMUNIKATIVE WERBUNG ART DIRECTOR: MICHAEL RÖSCH DESIGNER: CLAUDIA ANDERS DESCRIPTION: FOR A PHILANTHROPIC ORGANIZATION/FÜR EINE PHILANTROPISCHE GESELLSCHAFT/POUR UNE SOCIÉTÉ PHILANTHROPIQUE (GER)

1

2

3

4

5

■ **1.** Client: MASTER MINERALS Design Firm: LUGTU DURKEL Art Director/Designer: CAROL LUGTO DURKEL Description: FOR A SUPPLIER OF MINERALS AND CRYSTALS FOR "NEW AGE" USES/FÜR EINEN BIEFERANTEN VON MINERALIEN UND KRISTALLEN FÜR DEN "NEW AGE" BEDARF/POUR UN FOURNISSEUR IE MINÉRAUX ET DE CRISTAUX POUR LES BESOINS DU NEW AGE (USA) ■ **2.** Client: DENNISON STATIONERY PRODUCTS Design Firm: CROCKER INC. Art Director/Designer /Illustrator: BRUCE CROCKER Description: PRODUCT IDENTITY FOR A NEW PLASTIC PORTFO-LIO/PRODUKT-IDENTITÄT FÜR EINE NEUE/PLASTIKMAPPE/MARQUE D'IDENTIFICATION D'UN NOUVEAU PORTFOLIO EN PLASTIQUE (USA) ■ **3.** Client: BRIXTON POTTERY Design Firm: CLEAVER & ANDOR Art Director: PHIL CLEAVER Designers: PHIL CLEAVER/KAREN BILLINGHAM Description: FOR A POTTERY STUDIO/FÜR EINE TÖPFEREI/POUR UN ATELIER DE POTERIE (GBR) ■ **4.** Client: JÄRVAMAA ARENGUNÕUKOGU Design Firm: VAAL DESIGN Art Director/Designer: ANDREI KORMASOV Description: FOR THE COUNTY OF JÄRVAMAA IN ESTONIA/FÜR DAS GEBIET VON JÄRVAMAA IN ESTLAND/POUR LE DISTRICT DE JÄRVAMAA EN ESTONIE (USR) ■ **5.** Client: HISTOIRE CO., LTD. Design Firm: MICHIO MIYABAYASHI Art Director/Designer: MICHIO MIYABAYASHI (JPN)

1

■ 1. CLIENT: PHILLIP MORRIS, INC. DESIGN FIRM: THE DUFFY DESIGN GROUP ART DIRECTOR/DESIGNER:
CHARLES S. ANDERSON DESCRIPTION: PROPOSED LOGO FOR A NEW CIGARETTE/LOGO-ENTWURF FÜR
EINE NEUE ZIGARETTE/PROJET DE LOGO POUR UNE NOUVELLE MARQUE DE CIGARETTE (USA)

COLOR SECTION

FARBTEIL

PAGES EN COULEURS

1

■ 1. CLIENT: THE 21 CLUB DESIGN FIRM: PENTAGRAM DESIGN ART DIRECTORS: PETER HARRISON/SUSAN HOCHBAUM DESIGNER: SUSAN HOCHBAUM ILLUSTRATOR: PAUL DAVIS DESCRIPTION: PRIVATE CLUB AND RESTAU- RANT/FÜR EINEN PRIVAT-CLUB UND EIN RESTAURANT/POUR UN CLUB PRIVÉ DOUBLÉ D'UN RESTAURANT (USA)

1

2

3

■ 1. CLIENT: MUSICUM LAUDE DESIGN FIRM: THE WELLER INSTITUTE FOR THE CURE OF DESIGN, INC. ART DIRECTOR/DESIGNER/ILLUSTRATOR: DON WELLER DESCRIPTION: FOR PRODUCERS OF MUSIC FOR TELE-VISION AND FILM/FÜR FORNSEH- UND FILM-MUSIKPRODUZENTEN/POUR DES PRODUCTEURS DE MUSIQUE POUR LA TV ET LE CINEMA (USA) ■ 2. CLIENT: DATACARD CORPORATION DESIGN FIRM: MCCOOL & COMPANY ART DIRECTOR/DESIGNER: DEB MINER DESCRIPTION: FOR A COMPUTER COMPANY'S ANNUAL SALES MEETING/POUR LA CONFÉRENCE DE VENTES ANNUELLE D'UN FABRICANT D'ORDINATEURS (USA) ■ 3. CLIENT: KAMIKAZE SKATEWEAR DESIGN FIRM: SABIN DESIGN ART DIRECTOR: GREG SABIN DESIGNER: TRACY SABIN ILLUSTRATOR: TRACY SABIN DESCRIPTION: FOR A SKATEBOARD CLOTHING COMPANY/FÜR EINEN HERSTELLER VON SKATEBOARD-MODE/POUR UN FABRICANT DE TENUES DE SKATEBOARD (USA)

4

5

6

■ 4. CLIENT: DICKSON'S INC. DESIGN FIRM: THE DUFFY DESIGN GROUP ART DIRECTOR: JOE DUFFY DESIGNER: SHARON WERNER ILLUSTRATOR: LYNN SCHULTE DESCRIPTION: SPECIALTY PRINTER/SPEZIAL-ISIERTE DRUCKEREI/IMPRIMEUR SPÉCIALISE (USA) ■ 5. CLIENT: PERET ASOCIADOS DESIGN FIRM: PERET ASOCIADOS ART DIRECTOR/DESIGNER/ILLUSTRATOR: PERET (SPA) ■ 6. CLIENT: MARGARET WATSON REPRESENTS DESIGN FIRM: PETERSON & COMPANY ART DIRECTOR/DESIGNER: BRYAN L. PETERSON DESCRIPTION: PHOTOGRAPHERS' REPRESENTATIVE/PHOTOGRAPHEN-AGENTUR/AGENCE DE PHOTOGRAPHES (USA)

1

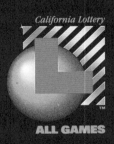

2

3

4

5

■ 1. CLIENT: WARNER BROS. RECORDS DESIGN FIRM: MARGO CHASE DESIGN ART DIRECTOR: JERI HEIDEN
DESIGNER: MARGO CHASE DESCRIPTION: FOR AN ALBUM RELEASE/FÜR EINE NEUE SCHALLPLATTE/POUR
UN NOUVEAU DISQUE (USA) ■ 2. CLIENT: CALIFORNIA STATE LOTTERY ART DIRECTOR: NICOLAS SID-
JAKOV DESIGNER/ILLUSTRATOR: MARK BERGMAN (USA) ■ 3. CLIENT: TRANSAMERICA DESIGN FIRM: SBG
PARTNERS ART DIRECTORS: NICOLAS SIDJAKOV/COURTNEY REESER DESIGNER: THOMAS BOND
DESCRIPTION: FOR A FINANCIAL CONGLOMERATE/FÜR EIN FINANZ-KONGLOMERAT/POUR UN CON-
GLOMÉRAT FINANCIER (USA) ■ 4. CLIENT: THE ART DEPARTMENT, A DIVISION OF CHARGO
PRINTING DESIGN FIRM: GRANDPRÉ AND WHALEY LTD. ART DIRECTOR/DESIGNER/ILLUSTRATOR: KEVIN
WHALEY DESCRIPTION: FOR THE DESIGN DIVISION OF A PRINTING COMPANY/FÜR DIE GRAPHIK-
ABTEILUNG EINER DRUCKEREI/POUR LE DEPARTEMENT GRAPHIQUE D'UNE IMPRIMERIE (USA) ■ 5.
CLIENT: BRIGHT LIGHTS DESIGN FIRM: PENTAGRAM DESIGN ART DIRECTOR/DESIGNER: WOODY PIRTLE (USA)

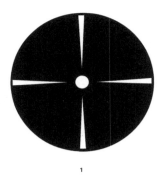

1

2

■ **1-4.** Client: SUNRISE DEPARTMENT STORES Design Firm: TERRELONGE DESIGN INC. Art Director/Designer: DEL TERRELONGE Description: FOR A CHAIN OF DEPARTMENT STORES; THE LOGO INCORPORATES TRADITIONAL IMAGES OF CHINESE CULTURE/FÜR EINE KAUFHAUSKETTE; DAS LOGO BASIERT AUF TRADITIONELLEN BILDERN DER CHINESISCHEN KULTUR/POUR UNE CHAINE DE GRADS MAGASINS; LE LOGO INTÉGRE DES IMAGES TRADITIONNELLES DE LA CIVILISATION CHINOISE (TAI)

3

4

1

2

3

■ **1.** CLIENT: MISTY ISLE FARMS DESIGN FIRM: HADW ART DIRECTOR: JACK ANDERSON DESIGNERS: JACK ANDERSON/JULIE TANAGI ILLUSTRATOR: MARY HERMES DESCRIPTION: FOR A PRODUCER OF HIGH-QUALITY BEEF/FÜR EINEN HERSTELLER ERSTKLASSIGER RINDFLEISCHPRODUKTE/POUR UN PRODUCTEUR DE VIANDE DE BOEUF DE PREMIERE QUALITÉ (USA) ■ **2.** CLIENT: THE HARRY LIME COMPANY DESIGN FIRM: COZZOLINO/ELLETT DESIGN D'VISION ART DIRECTOR: MIMMO COZZOLINO DESIGNER: ANDREW HOOK (AUS) ■ **3.** CLIENT: ULTRA LUCCA DELICATESSENS, INC. DESIGN FIRM: PRIMO ANGELI, INC. ART DIRECTOR: PRIMO ANGELI DESIGNERS: PRIMO ANGELI/MARK JONES DESCRIPTION: FOR AN IMPORTER OF ITALIAN WINES/FÜR EINEN IMPORTEUR ITALIENISCHER WEINE/POUR UN IMPORTATEUR DE VINS ITALIENS (USA)

INDEX

VERZEICHNIS

INDEX

CALL FOR ENTRIES

EINLADUNG

APPEL D'ENVOIS

CALL FOR ENTRIES

GRAPHIS DESIGN 93

ENTRY DEADLINE: NOVEMBER 30, 1991

ADVERTISING: Newspaper and magazine. **DESIGN**: Promotion brochures, catalogs, invitations, record covers, announcements, logos and/or corporate campaigns, calendars, books, book covers, packaging (single or series, labels and/or complete packages). **EDITORIAL**: Company magazines, newspapers, consumer magazines, house organs, annual reports. **ILLUSTRATION**: All categories, black and white or color. **ELIGIBILITY**: All work produced between December 1, 1990 through November 30, 1991, as well as unpublished work from this period by professionals and students.

ANNUAL REPORTS 4

ENTRY DEADLINE: APRIL 30, 1992

All annual reports, capability brochures, public interest reports, and other corporate public relations material in a brochure format. **ELIGIBILITY**: All work published between April 30, 1991 and April 30, 1992.

GRAPHIS POSTER 93

ENTRY DEADLINE: APRIL 30, 1992

Cultural Posters: exhibitions, film, music theater, etc. Advertising Posters: consumer goods, self-promotion, etc. Social posters: education, conferences, and meetings, political, etc. **ELIGIBILITY**: All work produced between May 1, 1991 and April 30, 1992.

GRAPHIS PHOTO 93

ENTRY DEADLINE: JUNE 30, 1992

Advertising Photography: Ads, promotional brochure, catalogs, invitations, announcements, record covers, and calendars on all subjects. Editorial Photography: for press media (journalism and feature stories), books, corporate publications, etc. on all subjects. Fine Art Photography: Personal studies on all subjects. Unpublished Photography: Experimental and student work on all subjects. **ELIGIBILITY**: All work produced between July 1, 1991 and June 30, 1992.

RULES

By submitting work to **GRAPHIS**, the sender grants permission for his or her publication in any **GRAPHIS** book, as well as any article in **GRAPHIS** magazine, or any advertisement, brochure, or other printed matter produced specifically for the purpose of promoting the sale of these publications.

ELIGIBILITY: All work produced in the 12-month period previous to the submission deadlines, as well as rejected or unpublished work from this period, by professionals and students.

WHAT TO SEND: Please send the printed piece (unmounted but well protected). Do not send original art. For large, bulky or valuable pieces, please submit color photos or (duplicate) slides. **Entries cannot be returned.** Only in exceptional cases and by contacting us in advance will material be sent back.

HOW AND WHERE TO SEND: Please tape (do not glue) the entry form provided (or copy)–with full information–on the back of each piece. Entries can be sent by air mail, air parcel post or surface mail. Please do not send anything by air freight. Declare, "No Commercial Value" on packages, and label "Art for Contest." The number of transparencies and photos should be indicated on the parcel. (If sent by air courier, please mark "documents, Commercial Value 00.00.")

SINGLE ENTRY: North America: US $10.00 Germany: DM 10.00 All other countries: SFr. 10.00
FOR EACH CAMPAIGN ENTRY OF 3 OR MORE PIECES: North America: US $25.00 Germany: DM 25.00
All other countries: SFr 25.00

Please make checks payable to **GRAPHIS PRESS CORP. ZURICH** and include in parcel. These fees do not apply to students, if copy of student identification is included. (For entries from countries with exchange controls, please contact us.) A confirmation of receipt will be sent to each entrant, and all entrants will be notified whether or not their work has been accepted for publication. By submitting work you qualify for a 25% discount on the purchase of the respective book. Thank you for you entry.

GRAPHIS PRESS CORP. 107 DUFOURSTRASSE CH-8008 ZURICH, SWITZERLAND

EINLADUNG
. . . .

GRAPHIS DESIGN 93

EINSENDESCHLUSS: 30. NOVEMBER 1991

WERBUNG: In Zeitungen und Zeitschriften. **DESIGN**: Werbeprospekte, Kataloge, Einladungen, Schallplattenhüllen, Anzeigen, Signete und/oder Image-Kampagnen, Kalender, Bücher, Buchumschläge, Packungen. **REDAKTIONELLES DESIGN**: Firmenpublikationen, Zeitungen, Zeitschriften, Jahresberichte. **ILLUSTRATION**: Alle Kategorien, schwarzweiss oder farbig. **IN FRAGE KOMMEN**: Alle Arbeiten von Fachleuten und Studenten - auch nicht publizierte. Arbeiten -, die zwischen Dezember 1990 und November 1991 entstanden sind.

ANNUAL REPORTS 4

EINSENDESCHLUSS: 30. APRIL 1992

Alle Jahresberichte einer Firma oder Organisation (Tabellen und Diagramme, Illustrationen und Photos). **IN FRAGE KOMMEN**: Alle Jahresberichte und ähnliche Firmenpublikationen für Öffentlichkeitsarbeit in Form von Broschüren von 1991 bis 1992.

GRAPHIS POSTER 93

EINSENDESCHLUSS: 30. APRIL 1992

KULTUR: Plakate für Ausstellungen, Film-, Theater- und Balletaufführungen usw. **WERBUNG**: Plakate für Konsumgüter, Eigenwerbung usw. **GESELLSCHAFT**: Plakate für Ausbildung, die Ankündigung von Tagungen usw. **IN FRAGE KOMMEN**: Alle Arbeiten, die zwischen Mai 1991 und April 1992 entstanden sind.

GRAPHIS PHOTO 93

EINSENDESCHLUSS: 30. JUNI 1992

Werbephotographie: Anzeigen, Prospekte, Kataloge, Einladungen, Bekanntmachungen, Schallplattenhüllen, Kalender. Redaktionelle Photographie: Pressephotos, Firmenpublikationen usw. In den Bereichen Mode, Architektur, Kunst, Natur, Wissenschaft und Technik, Alltag, Sport, Porträts, Stilleben usw. Künstlerische Photographie: Persönliche Studien. Unveröffentlichte Aufnahmen: Experimentelle Photographie und Arbeiten von Studenten und Schülern. **IN FRAGE KOMMEN**: Alle Arbeiten, die zwischen Juli 1991 und Juni 1992 entstanden sind.

TEILNAHMEBEDINGUNGEN

GRAPHIS erhält die Erlaubnis zur Veröffentlichung der eingesandten Arbeiten sowohl im entsprechenden Jahrbuch als auch in der Zeitschrift **GRAPHIS** oder für die Wiedergabe im Zusammenhang mit
. . . .

IN FRAGE KOMMEN: Alle Arbeiten von Fachleuten und Studenten - auch nicht publizierte Arbeiten -, welche in den zwölf Monaten vor Einsendeschluss entstanden sind.
. . . .

WAS EINSENDEN: Bitte senden Sie uns das gedruckte Beispiel (gut geschützt). Senden Sie keine Originale. Bei unhandlichen, umfangreichen und wertvollen Sendungen bitten wir um Farbphotos oder Duplikat-Dias.
. . . .

WIE SCHICKEN: Bitte befestigen Sie das vorgesehene Etikett (oder Kopie) - vollständig ausgefüllt - mit Klebstreifen (nicht mit Klebstoff) auf der Rückseite jeder Arbeit. Bitte per Luftpost oder auf normalem Postweg einsenden. **Keine Luftfrachtsendungen.** Deklarieren Sie «ohn jeden Handelswert» und «Arbeitsproben für Wettbewerb». Die Anzahl der Dias und Photos sollte auf dem Paket angegeben werden (bei Luftkurier-Sendungen vermerken Sie «Dokumente, ohne jeden Handelswert»).
. . . .

SFR. 10.--/DM 10.-- FUR EINZELNE ARBEITEN
SFR. 25.--/DM 25.-- FÜR KAMPAGNEN ODER SERIEN (MEHR ALS 3 STÜCK)
Bitte senden Sie uns einen Scheck (SFr.-Schecks bitte auf eine Schweizer Bank ziehen) oder überweisen Sie den Betrag auf PC Zürich 80-23071-9 oder PSchK Frankfurt 3000 57-602. Diese Gebühren gelten nicht für Studenten. Senden Sie bitte eine Kopie des Studentenausweises. (Für Einsendungen aus Ländern mit Devisenbeschränkungen bitten wir Sie, uns zu kontaktieren.) Jeder Einsender erhält eine Empfangsbestätigung und wird über Erscheinen oder Nichterscheinen seiner Arbeit informiert. Durch Ihre Einsendung erhalten Sie 25% Rabatt auf das betreffende Buch. Herzlichen Dank für Ihre Mitarbeit.

GRAPHIS VERLAG AG, DUFOURSTRASSE 107 CH-8008 ZURICH, SCHWEIZ

APPEL D'ENVOIS

GRAPHIS DESIGN 93

DATE LIMITE D'ENVOI: 30 NOVEMBRE 1992

PUBLICITÉ: journaux, magazines. **DESIGN**: brochures de promotion, catalogues, invitations, pochettes de disques, annonces, emblèmes, en-têtes, campagnes de prestige, calendriers, livres, jaquettes, emballages (spécimen ou série, étiquettes ou emballages complets). **DESIGN ÉDITORIAL**: magazines de sociétés, journaux, revues, rapports annuels. **ILLUSTRATION**: toutes catégories en noir et blanc ou en couleurs. **ADMISSION**: Tous les travaux réalisés entre décembre 1990 et novembre 1991 par des professionnels ou étudiants, ainsi que les travaux refusés ou non publiés durant cette période.

ANNUAL REPORTS 4

DATE LIMITE D'ENVOI: 30 AVRIL 1992

Tous travaux publiés en relation avec le rapport annuel d'une entreprise ou d'une organisation. **ADMISSION**: Tous les rapports annuels et autre rapports destinés au grand public publiés sous forme de brochure en 1991 ou en 1992.

GRAPHIS POSTER 93

DATE LIMITE D'ENVOI: 30 AVRIL 1992

AFFICHES CULTURELLES: expositions, film, théâtre, ballet, concerts etc. **AFFICHES PUBLICITAIRES**: produits de consommation, autopromotion, etc. **AFFICHES SOCIALES**: formation, conférences et annonces de manifestations ou de réunions politiques, etc. **ADMISSION**: Tous les travaux réalisés entre mai 1991 et avril 1992.

GRAPHIS PHOTO 93

DATE LIMITE D'ENVOI: 30 JUIN 1992

PHOTO PUBLICITAIRE: annonces, brochures de promotion, catalogues, pochettes de disques, calendriers. **PHOTO RÉDACTIONNELLE**: reportages, livres, publications d'entreprises, etc. dans les domaines suivants: mode, arts, architecture, nature, sciences, techniques, vie quotidienne, sports, portraits, nature morte, etc. **PHOTO D'ART**: études personnelles. **PHOTOS NON-PUBLIÉES**: travaux expérimentaux et projets d'étudiants. **ADMISSION**: Les travaux réalisés entre juillet 91 et juin 92.

MODALITÉS D'ENVOI

Par votre envoi, vous donnez expressément à **GRAPHIS** l'autorisation de reproduire les travaux reçus aussi bien dans le livre en question que dans le magazine **GRAPHIS**, ou dans tout imprimé concernant des comptes rendus ou du matériel publicitaire sur les publications **GRAPHIS**.

ADMISSION: Sont acceptés tous les travaux de professionnels et d'étudiants - même inédits - réalisés pendant les douze mois précédant le délai limite d'envoi.

QUE NOUS ENVOYER: Veuillez nous envoyer un exemplaire imprimé. N'envoyez pas d'originaux. Pour les travaux de grand format, volumineux ou de valeur, veuillez nous envoyer des photos ou des duplicata. **Veuillez noter que les travaux ne peuvent pas être retournés,** sauf dans des cas exceptionnels et si vous

COMMENT ET OU ENVOYER: Veuillez scotcher (ne pas coller) au dos de chaque spécimen les étiquettes ci-jointes (ou photocopies) dûment remplies. Envoyez les travaux de préférence par avion, ou par voie de surface. **Ne nous envoyez rien en fret aérien.** Indiquez «Sans aucune valeur commerciale» et «Echantillons de spécimens pour concours». Le nombre de diapositives et de photos doit être indiqué sur le paquet. (Pour les envois par courrier, inscrire «Documents, sans aucune valeur commerciale».)

SFR. 10.00 pour les envois concernant un seul travail
SFR. 25.00 pour chaque série de 3 travaux ou davantage
Veuillez joindre à votre envoi un chèque tiré sur une banque suisse ou verserez ce montant au compte chèque postal Zurich 80.23071.9. Les étudiants sont exemptés de cette taxe. Prière de joindre une photocopie de la carte d'étudiant. (Si vous résidez dans un pays qui connaît le contrôle des changes, veuillez nous contacter préalablement.) Nous vous ferons parvenir un accusé de réception. Vous serez informé par la suite de la parution ou non-parution de vos travaux. Votre envoi vous vaudra une réduction de 25% sur l'annuel en question. Veuillez faire parvenir vos travaux à l'adresse suivante:

ÉDITIONS GRAPHIS, DUFOURSTRASSE 107 CH-8008 ZURICH, SWITZERLAND

BOOKS	USA	CANADA
☐ GRAPHIS PHOTO 91	US$69	US$ 94
☐ GRAPHIS POSTER 91	US$69	US$ 94
☐ GRAPHIS DESIGN 91	US$69	US$ 94
☐ GRAPHIS LETTERHEAD 1	US$69	US$ 94
☐ GRAPHIS LOGO 1	US$50	US$ 70
☐ THE GRAPHIC DESIGNER'S GREEN BOOK	US$25	US$ 41
☐ GRAPHIS PHOTO 90	US$69	US$ 94
☐ GRAPHIS ANNUAL REPORTS 2	US$75	US$100
☐ GRAPHIS POSTER 90	US$69	US$ 94
☐ GRAPHIS CORPORATE IDENTITY 1	US$75	US$100
☐ GRAPHIS PHOTO 89	US$65	US$ 91
☐ GRAPHIS PACKAGING 5	US$75	US$100
☐ GRAPHIS DIAGRAM 1	US$65	US$ 91
☐ GRAPHIS ANNUAL REPORTS 1	US$65	US$ 91

☐ CHECK ENCLOSED (GRAPHIS AGREES TO PAY MAILING COSTS)

☐ BILL ME (MAILING COSTS IN ADDITION TO ABOVE
BOOK PRICE WILL BE CHARGED, BOOK(S) WILL BE SENT
WHEN PAYMENT IS RECEIVED)

PLEASE PRINT

NAME   DATE

TITLE

COMPANY

ADDRESS

CITY   POSTAL CODE

STATE/PROVINCE

COUNTRY

SIGNATURE   DATE

PLEASE SEND ORDER FORM AND MAKE CHECK PAYABLE TO:

GRAPHIS US, INC.141 LEXINGTON AVENUE, NEW YORK, NY 10016, USA

. . . .

REQUEST FOR CALL FOR ENTRIES

PLEASE PUT ME ON THE "CALL FOR ENTRIES" LIST FOR THE FOLLOWING TITLES:

☐ GRAPHIS DESIGN   ☐ GRAPHIS ANNUAL REPORTS

☐ GRAPHIS DIAGRAM   ☐ GRAPHIS CORPORATE IDENTITY

☐ GRAPHIS POSTER   ☐ GRAPHIS PHOTO

☐ GRAPHIS PACKAGING   ☐ GRAPHIS LETTERHEAD

☐ GRAPHIS LOGO

SUBMITTING MATERIAL TO ANY OF THE ABOVE TITLES, QUALIFIES SENDER FOR A
25% DISCOUNT TOWARD PURCHASE OF THAT TITLE.

BOOKS	BRD	WORLD	U.K.
☐ GRAPHIS PHOTO 91	DM149,-	SFR.123.-	£49.00
☐ GRAPHIS POSTER 91	DM149,-	SFR.123.	£49.00
☐ GRAPHIS DESIGN 91	DM149,-	SFR.123.-	£49.00
☐ GRAPHIS LETTERHEAD 1	DM149,-	SFR.123.-	£49.00
☐ GRAPHIS LOGO 1	DM108,-	SFR. 92.-	£36.00
☐ THE GRAPHIC DESIGNER'S GREEN BOOK	DM 54,-	SFR. 46.-	£18.00
☐ GRAPHIS PHOTO 90	DM149,-	SFR.123.-	£49.00
☐ GRAPHIS ANNUAL REPORTS 2	DM162,-	SFR.137.-	£52.00
☐ GRAPHIS POSTER 90	DM149,-	SFR.123.-	£49.00
☐ GRAPHIS CORPORATE IDENTITY 1	DM160,-	SFR.132.-	£48.00
☐ GRAPHIS PHOTO 89	DM148,-	SFR.118.-	£46.50
☐ GRAPHIS PACKAGING 5	DM160,-	SFR.132.-	£48.00
☐ GRAPHIS DIAGRAM 1	DM138,-	SFR.112.-	£45.00
☐ GRAPHIS ANNUAL REPORTS 1	DM138,-	SFR.112.-	£45.00

☐ CHECK ENCLOSED (FOR EUROPE, PLEASE MAKE SFR, CHECKS
PAYABLE TO A SWISS BANK)
☐ AMOUNT PAID INTO GRAPHIS ACCOUNT AT THE UNION BANK
OF SWITZERLAND, ACCT NO 3620063 IN ZÜRICH.
☐ AMOUNT PAID TO POSTAL CHEQUE ACCOUNT ZÜRICH 80-23071-9 (THROUGH YOUR
LOCAL POST OFFICE)
☐ PLEASE BILL ME (MAILING COSTS IN ADDITION TO ABOVE BOOK PRICE WILL BE
CHARGED, BOOK(S) WILL BE SENT WHEN PAYMENT IS RECEIVED)

PLEASE PRINT

NAME   DATE
_____

TITLE
_____

COMPANY
_____

ADDRESS
_____

CITY   POSTAL CODE
_____

STATE/PROVINCE
_____

COUNTRY
_____

SIGNATURE   DATE

PLEASE SEND ORDER FORM AND MAKE CHECK PAYABLE TO:
GRAPHIS PRESS CORP,. DUFOURSTRASSE 107, CH-8008 ZÜRICH, SWITZERLAND

REQUEST FOR CALL FOR ENTRIES
PLEASE PUT ME ON THE "CALL FOR ENTRIES" LIST FOR THE FOLLOWING TITLES:

☐ GRAPHIS DESIGN   ☐ GRAPHIS ANNUAL REPORTS
☐ GRAPHIS DIAGRAM   ☐ GRAPHIS CORPORATE IDENTITY
☐ GRAPHIS POSTER   ☐ GRAPHIS PHOTO
☐ GRAPHIS PACKAGING   ☐ GRAPHIS LETTERHEAD
☐ GRAPHIS LOGO

SUBMITTING MATERIAL TO ANY OF THE ABOVE TITLES, QUALIFIES SENDER FOR A 25%
DISCOUNT TOWARD PURCHASE OF THAT TITLE.

MAGAZINE   **USA**   **CANADA**

☐ NEW ☐ RENEW

☐ TWO YEARS (12 ISSUES)   US$149.00   US$166.00

☐ ONE YEAR (6 ISSUES)   US$ 79.00   US$ 88.00

☐ 25% DISCOUNT FOR STUDENTS WITH COPY OF VALID,

DATED STUDENT ID AND PAYMENT WITH ORDER

FOR CREDIT CARD PAYMENT:

☐ VISA ☐ MASTERCARD

ACCT. NO

                                EXP. DATE

SIGNATURE

☐ CHECK ENCLOSED ☐ BILL ME

CHECK THE LANGUAGE VERSION DESIRED:

☐ ENGLISH ☐ GERMAN ☐ FRENCH

PLEASE PRINT

NAME

                                DATE

TITLE

COMPANY

ADDRESS

CITY   **POSTAL CODE**

STATE/PROVINCE

COUNTRY

PLEASE SEND ORDER FORM AND MAKE CHECK PAYABLE TO:

GRAPHIS US, INC., P.O. BOX 3063 SOUTHEASTERN, PA 19398-3063

SERVICE WILL BEGIN WITH ISSUE THAT IS CURRENT

WHEN ORDER IS PROCESSED (LOGO 1)

REQUEST FOR CALL FOR ENTRIES

PLEASE PUT ME ON THE "CALL FOR ENTRIES" LIST FOR THE FOLLOWING TITLES:

☐ GRAPHIS DESIGN   ☐ GRAPHIS ANNUAL REPORTS

☐ GRAPHIS DIAGRAM   ☐ GRAPHIS CORPORATE IDENTITY

☐ GRAPHIS POSTER   ☐ GRAPHIS PHOTO

☐ GRAPHIS PACKAGING   ☐ GRAPHIS LETTERHEAD

☐ GRAPHIS LOGO

SUBMITTING MATERIAL TO ANY OF THE ABOVE TITLES, QUALIFIES SENDER FOR A 25%

DISCOUNT TOWARD PURCHASEOF THAT TITLE.

MAGAZINE	BRD	WORLD	U.K.

☐ NEW ☐ RENEW

| ☐ TWO YEARS (12 ISSUES) | DM305,- | SFR262.- | £102.00 |
| ☐ ONE YEAR (6 ISSUES) | DM162,- | SFR140.- | £ 54.00 |

☐ 25% DISCOUNT FOR STUDENTS WITH COPY OF VALID,

DATED STUDENT ID AND PAYMENT WITH ORDER

SUBSCRIPTION FEES INCLUDE POSTAGE TO ANY PART OF THE WORLD. AIRMAIL

AVAILABLE EVERYWHERE EXCEPT EUROPE

AND NORTH AMERICA.

☐ AIRMAIL SURCHARGE (6 ISSUES)   SFR 58.-

FOR CREDIT CARD PAYMENT:

(ALL CARDS DEBITED IN SWISS FRANCS):

☐ AMERICAN EXPRESS ☐ DINER'S CLUB ☐ EURO/MASTERCARD

☐ VISA/BARCLAY/CARTE BLEUE

ACCT. NO   EXP. DATE

SIGNATURE   CARDHOLDER NAME

☐ CHECK ENCLOSED ☐ BILL ME

CHECK THE LANGUAGE VERSION DESIRED:

☐ ENGLISH ☐ GERMAN ☐ FRENCH

PLEASE PRINT

NAME   DATE

TITLE

COMPANY

ADDRESS

CITY   POSTAL CODE

STATE/PROVINCE

COUNTRY

PLEASE SEND ORDER FORM AND MAKE CHECK PAYABLE TO:

GRAPHIS PRESS CORP.,

DUFOURSTRASSE 107 CH-8008 ZÜRICH, SWITZERLAND

SERVICE WILL BEGIN WITH ISSUE THAT IS CURRENT

WHEN ORDER IS PROCESSED (LOGO 1)

REQUEST FOR CALL FOR ENTRIES

PLEASE PUT ME ON THE "CALL FOR ENTRIES" LIST FOR THE FOLLOWING TITLES:

☐ GRAPHIS DESIGN   ☐ GRAPHIS ANNUAL REPORTS

☐ GRAPHIS DIAGRAM   ☐ GRAPHIS CORPORATE IDENTITY

☐ GRAPHIS POSTER   ☐ GRAPHIS PHOTO

☐ GRAPHIS PACKAGING   ☐ GRAPHIS LETTERHEAD

☐ GRAPHIS LOGO

SUBMITTING MATERIAL TO ANY OF THE ABOVE TITLES, QUALIFIES SENDER FOR A

25% DISCOUNT TOWARD PURCHASE OF THAT TITLE.